Myself Resolved

AN ARTIST'S EXPERIENCE WITH LYMPHOMA

By Darcy Lynn

FOREWORD BY MARIE BAKITAS WHEDON

MENISCUS HEALTH CARE COMMUNICATIONS
DIVISION OF MENISCUS LIMITED

PHILADELPHIA, PENNSYLVANIA

Library of Congress Cataloging in Publication Data
Lynn, Darcy, 1956-
Myself resolved: an artist's experience with lymphoma / by Darcy Lynn;
introduction by Marie Bakitas Whedon.
p. cm
ISBN 0-940977-06-0 (pbk.)
1. Lynn, Darcy, 1956—Health. 2. Lymphoma—Patients—New York
(N.Y.)—Biography. 3. Artists—New York (N.Y.)—Biography.
I. Title.
[DNLM: 1. Lynn, Darcy, 1956–. 2. Lymphoma, Non-Hodgkin's—
personal narratives. 3. Professional-Patient Relations—personal narratives.
4. Art Therapy. WH 525 L989m 1994]
RC280.L9L95 1994
362.1'9699446—dc20
[B]
DNLM/DLC
for Library of Congress 94-36580 CIP

Published by Lois Trench-Hines
Edited by Nancy C. Phillips
Copy edited by Leslie Fenton
Proofreading by Tom Gibbons
Cover/interior design by Susan Kidney
Photography by Fran Miller Smith
Production assistance by Nancy L. Matteo and Frances Rosato
Technical assistance by Alan Sobkowiak

Publication of this book was made possible by a grant from
Cerenex™ Pharmaceuticals, division of Glaxo Inc.
Five Moore Drive
Research Triangle Park, NC 27709

Published and distributed internationally by
Meniscus Health Care Communications
Division of Meniscus Limited
107 North 22nd Street, Suite 200
Philadelphia, PA 19103-1302

Printed in the United States of America on recycled paper

♻

To Cynthia,
who gave me the gift of life
and the gift of art

Acknowledgments

In creating this book I wish to acknowledge the support, encouragement, and love from my family and friends (an extra special thank you to Amy) and the valuable assistance from Gloria, David, Donna, and especially Lydia. Also, my thanks to Marie and to everyone at Meniscus Limited who made this possible; as well as to Cerenex Pharmaceuticals, division of Glaxo Inc., whose generous financial support helped bring this book to fruition.

Foreword

Marie Bakitas Whedon

There are moments in life when an ordinary event or chance meeting can result in extraordinary outcomes. This is what I think about the collaboration through many projects I have enjoyed with Darcy Lynn. The combination of a nurse/writer-wanna-be-artist and artist-not-wanna-be-patient formed a perfect union for accomplishing our mutual goals. As a nurse and author interested in quality of life, I wished to communicate to my colleagues the importance of the human experience of illness. Darcy, as an artist with lymphoma, wished to process her illness and to seek an avenue through which to share this experience with others. I think this book accomplishes both.

The first time I met Darcy was at the Dartmouth-Hitchcock Medical Center's inaugural Cancer Survivor's Day celebration. A Cancer Center staff member had brought Darcy's name to us, having heard about her from a "friend of a friend," as a possible speaker. She was described as an artist and cancer survivor from New York City who "painted her way through her disease." As the day for the big event approached, a poster that Darcy had sent with some of her work was circulating to members of the planning group. Slight panic spread when we saw that some of the paintings were nudes. A few members of the planning committee were a little nervous that someone might be offended. (I'm sure that other "politically correct" conference planners can appreciate this concern.) Should she be asked not to include these, even though they were, in our opinion, her most dramatic work? Luckily, good sense prevailed and Darcy was allowed to be Darcy.

Fears vanished and awe struck as she told her story and showed her paintings (especially the nudes). She seemed a little nervous at first. But she spoke plainly and immediately put the audience at ease as she talked to them, not at them. For the next 30 minutes, Darcy described her struggle and recovery from cancer. Except for an occasional exclamatory "Oh!" as each new painting was revealed in the sequence of her story, the overflowing room of 400 survivors was silent.

The first time you meet Darcy after seeing her work, you might be startled. Her appearance is not quite what you might expect (don't worry, though—this amuses Darcy). She is petite, soft-spoken, gentle, and very young-looking. You might think, "How can such powerful work have been created by such an unassuming-looking woman?" As you come to know her, it is no longer surprising.

Myself Resolved: An Artist's Experience With Lymphoma is the story of one woman's struggle to maintain her personhood and integrity in the midst of life-threatening illness. Darcy tells us her story in words, and her experience and feelings through images. Although her story is unique, it communicates some universal messages. I say this because I have had multiple opportunities to see patients', survivors', and health professionals' reactions to her work. Patients and survivors often say, "Yes, that is just how I felt—dehumanized, bare," and some, "healed." They find comfort, solace, and reconciliation in knowing that someone has finally captured what it is really like to experience the trauma of cancer treatment. Finally someone has expressed what they could not. Young and old, men and women—all can identify.

Responses from health care professionals vary. Some feel shock, embarrassment, or guilt because the vivid images reflect some of what we have caused with our treatments. Others find the depth of meaning to be breathtaking and moving. One surprising response came from a professional who said, "Aren't you afraid that if you show these to other patients, it might frighten them?" (as though they have not already felt the fear of cancer).

The powerful intimacy of her work goes beyond that of nudity of the human body. The presence of a Hickman catheter, radiation markings, and scars strewn around her breasts reveal not only the body, but the spirit and the soul. It is an awkward contrast, juxtaposing the foreign "healing" devices and marks against a bare, frail body. The other symbols of how she viewed her treatment experiences and her health care providers are revealing and instructive. I think many feel honored by the tribute she has paid them on canvas. Some of Darcy's verbal descriptions and stories will sound very familiar; her paintings make you feel—pain, humility, and hope. Her line drawings are fun, carefree, and mischievous and share some lighter impressions of her illness. Patients going through the ups and downs of steroid therapy will certainly be able to relate to "Bug-eyed Darcy on prednisone" (page 51). These are important moments to remember as well.

Susan Bond Muir, MA, an art therapist and art therapy consultant in New Hampshire, describes the potential healing of art therapy in this way:

> *Art therapy allows individuals to use art as a means of self-expression: to reconcile emotional conflicts and to foster self-awareness and personal growth. Thus, through the creative process, individuals under physical, emotional and/or spiritual stress can work through and integrate their situations to facilitate healing. The creative process is one which is naturally healing; therefore the benefits and possibilities of using art therapy with people under stress can be profound [personal communication].*

For Darcy this was partly therapy, but more an affirmation of life and who she is as a person. It is not surprising that Darcy had some trouble showing her work in the galleries of the "not yet sick." (This is what Paul Cowan, a former patient and writer from New York, calls healthy people.) It can be frightening to be so vividly reminded of our vulnerability. But it is reassuring to know that one is not alone and that one's experience can be seen, heard, and understood.

The goal of this project was to provide a vehicle for communication between patients and health care providers about the experience of illness and how it is affected by the particular disease, treatments, and providers of care. I think this goal has been met. However, it would not have been met without the support of others who also shared this vision. I would like to acknowledge and thank the leaders and staff of Meniscus Limited (Nancy, Lois, and others), who supported and encouraged us in our vision to share this work with a larger audience than could be reached through live presentations. I also wish to thank the leaders and representatives at Cerenex Pharmaceuticals, especially Tim Arendt, for demonstrating, once again, a commitment to valuing and improving the patient's experience throughout cancer treatment.

Marie Bakitas Whedon, MS, RN, OCN
Hematology/Oncology
Clinical Nurse Specialist
Dartmouth-Hitchcock Medical Center
Lebanon, New Hampshire, 1994

*P*reface

Darcy Lynn

This is the story of my experience with the cancer lymphoma—the adventures and thoughts I had during my illness, treatments, and recovery.

I fought my illness with the best weapon I had—my art. I've been painting almost all my life after starting to draw at the age of two. I was born into art; my mother is an artist and so was her father. I don't believe I ever wished to be anything other than an artist. I painted to give definition and meaning to my illness. It was a way for me to translate all I did not understand, and more importantly, it was a way to gain control over my illness. No one could tell me what or how to paint. It was up to me to express on the canvas how I felt.

My family played a crucial part in my recovery. We are very close to one another, and they are part of me. In order to protect their privacy, there are no descriptions or paintings of them. Those I did paint are people from the outside who came into my life and illness to help me fight. (All the doctor's names have been changed to protect their privacy.) The dialogues with my doctors are as I remember them.

Many people whom I don't mention played a part in my recovery, no matter how small—other friends, relatives, nurses, technicians, and doctors' secretaries, who encouraged me to fight.

As you will see, I am also a strong believer in humor and imagination, and my ability to laugh at my predicaments, to see the absurd side of life, made it all the easier to cope.

You will note that *The Lymphoma Series*, which is what I call the paintings, is set in the back of the book. The paintings are not grouped chronologically, but by the categories I chose to show the unity of the works: Images From the Hospital, My Body During Treatment, Portraits, and Recovery.

This is not a "how to" book. I don't believe I have a method or solution for coping with cancer, because each person's circumstances are different. Many people don't wish to relate to their doctors as I have to mine, or have the urge to paint their experiences.

My reason for telling this story is to share it with those who have survived cancer or any grave illness or with people who have helped a loved one go through it. I want them to know that they are not alone. I also hope that members of the medical profession will find it useful to see another perspective. Here then is my story, complete with paintings and drawings.

Contents

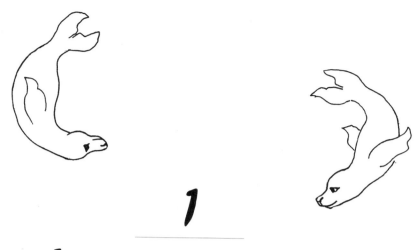

1

Descent and the Climb Back Up

I first noticed my shortness of breath while climbing the steep hills of Seattle in early November 1990. This was just two months after my 34th birthday. Believing it was due to my depression, I paid it no notice. I had just been laid off from a job I hated, although it provided me with the means to survive, and was bitterly disappointed with my life in this city. My mother, my brother Casey (also an artist), and I had moved to Seattle from New York City, hoping to find a cleaner, safer city where we could live and create art, but this was not to be.

My mother and I moved back to New York in January 1991. She returned to a former job of teaching writing skills in a university in New Jersey. I hoped to find a job in New York City. We left Casey with great reluctance. He would return in April, driving in a rented moving truck with the rest of our belongings. His only companion on this cross-country trip would be his new puppy, Ringo.

I spent the next three months in New York City, searching for a job and moving from place to place. I suffered bouts of flu, jaw pain from gritting my teeth in my sleep, and other discomforts but still believed it was all psychological. Meanwhile, my shortness of breath grew worse. I went to my physician, Dr. Douglas, three or four times but never fully voiced my true ailments.

Depression and ill health deepened, and I finally moved to my mother's tiny apartment in New Jersey. My money and health were almost depleted. I made another visit to Dr. Douglas, as my breathing had become more difficult. He took x-rays of my chest and immediately sent me to get CAT scans (sectional three-dimensional x-rays) of my chest and to see a specialist; my lungs were filling with fluid.

A few days later I went to see the specialist with my CAT scans; my sister Cilla and my mother accompanied me. We sat in a tiny waiting room for some time until a large man with jet-black hair parted in the middle above a wide face came out of

Dr. Douglas (My General Practitioner)
Oil on canvas. 1991. 14" x 22"

the office. He wore bright red suspenders and a bow tie. This was the specialist, Dr. Loblolly. He ushered my mother and me into a dark office, put my CAT scans on the light box, and showed us seats. After looking at the scans, he said, "Lymphoma or Hodgkin's disease—you do not have cancer. It's a tumor—a liquid tumor—that needs to be treated with radiation." He turned to me and said, "Nor would it have mattered if you'd come in earlier, the treatment would've been the same."

He sat down, separated from us by a heavy wooden desk, and continued to foretell my future. "I want to put you in the clinic at the hospital here in New York City so that I can perform a bronchoscopy and a biopsy. The bronchoscopy will require putting a tube down your throat. For the biopsy I will stick a tube in the chest pleural cavity around your left lung—it seems to be filled the most—to drain it off."

"What is the clinic?" asked my mother.

"It is similar to a hotel setting, with one floor devoted to hospital care. A care partner stays with the patient. I suppose that would be you," he said as he looked at her. "Tests are performed in the clinic, treatment for people on intravenous medications, anything not requiring total hospitalization."

As I sat in my chair trying to absorb all this horrible news, I stared at this big man and felt myself sinking downward. I had a really bad illness. Wasn't it cancer? I had never been in the hospital before. Well, at least I'd have my mother with me. I had to steel myself for a very big fight. Dr. Loblolly looked at the CAT scans again and said, "Lots of people live with only one lung, so don't worry!"

I turned to look at the scans to see one lung filled completely and the other filling fast. How would I survive on half a lung? Abruptly he turned to me with an expression close to animosity. "Now I don't want to hear any talk of this being your fault or any of that guilt trip stuff, or see this?" He waved one large fist at me. "I'll punch you in the face if I do!"

Well, that was damned reassuring! I was drowning in pain and fear and he was lecturing me on guilt? I wanted help as my sense of isolation and terror grew, but he was so intimidating that I shrank under his gaze. The Great Oz had spoken.

We waited for five days to check into the clinic. During that time I saw Paul

Tsongas, 1992 presidential candidate, on television, and he spoke of his battle with the cancer lymphoma. I clung to Dr. Loblolly's words (that I didn't have cancer) but could not convince myself of their validity. I asked myself, "Are there two kinds of lymphoma—cancerous and noncancerous?" I wasn't to confront the answer to this question for several weeks.

The night before check-in day, I could barely breathe lying down, and many thoughts of cancer and death entered my head. How would I fight this illness? Where was the help I needed?

Start of the Descent ～ It was nightmarish. We checked into the clinic, and many tests were performed. The worst was a CAT scan of my abdomen, which required me to drink a lot of orange-flavored liquid beforehand. This was difficult because I had reached the point at which I could hardly drink anything, and I had given up eating. Luckily, the results were good; the lymphoma had not spread to my stomach. Night came, and I spent it curled in a fetal position on my right side, the only way I could breathe.

The next day, Monday, was doctor-and-draining day. Dr. Loblolly called me to the main floor to do the procedure. My mother and my sister Lydia went with me; I traveled in a wheelchair, as walking had become difficult.

"Now what's all this?" asked Dr. Loblolly. "Why the wheelchair?"

I grinned sheepishly and said nothing. Lydia wheeled me into a tiny examining room, where I climbed onto an examination table. Dr. Loblolly came in behind me and closed the door while Lydia and my mother waited outside. He put a tape into a cassette player, saying, "I brought a tape for you. I think music helps a patient to relax."

"Is it classical music or the Beatles?" I asked.

"Neither, but I think you will like it. Now roll up the back of your shirt so I can insert the tube through this syringe into your left chest cavity." The music started, and it sounded like Cyndi Lauper—loud and jarring. I saw the tube, which had a bag attached to the end. I turned my head to look out the window. He continued, "After a while it will begin to hurt and you will cough. That is when I will stop. We could ask a nurse to come in and hold your hand." He looked at me, smirking, and said, "Naw, you won't need it. All right, I've got the tube in and fluid is coming out."

I sat still, feeling the tube insertion and the fluid being sucked out. I grew scared and fought to keep calm and still. Dr. Loblolly continued to talk about himself and his methods, and I grunted my replies. All of a sudden it hurt inside. I felt as if my lung had caved in and I coughed. I forgot all he had said earlier and was sure he had done something wrong.

There was a hurried knock at the door, and the short, sturdy figure of Dr. Douglas appeared. He rushed in—to my complete surprise and relief—with a look of grave concern on his usually jovial face. "Hello, Dr. Loblolly. What music are you playing?" He looked me in the eye, trying to decipher my feelings. "How are you, Darcy?" I just smiled feebly as my eyes began to brim with tears. I was too embarrassed to cry but afraid I would if I spoke. I was so glad to see him. Now in his fifties, he had been my physician for 15 years. He was a warm, fatherly man, not much taller than I, with deep brown eyes. He always made me feel safe and secure.

"Look at all I got out of her left lung!" exclaimed Dr. Loblolly as he held up the bag. It was about a foot long and six inches in diameter, filled with yellow-brown lymphoma muck. "I would have got more but she coughed—still, this is not bad." He held it up like a schoolboy with a prize, not like a doctor of 45 or so. He exchanged a few more words with Dr. Douglas, who patted my knee just before he left. I was sorry to see him go.

For my next test, Lydia wheeled me into another examining room with my CAT scans, x-rays from Dr. Douglas' office, and a test tube of lymphoma muck. Into the room walked a quiet, calm man of medium height and build, about age 40, and wearing a doctor's lab coat. "Hello, I am Dr. Barnes. I am going to perform a bone marrow biopsy on you to make sure the lymphoma has not spread to your bone marrow." His gentle, intelligent face and composed manner soothed me. Here was someone who knew what he was doing. I rolled over on my right side and faced the wall, pulling down my pants with some difficulty. I felt rather weak. "It will only hurt for a few seconds. I will count to 10 so you can prepare." He stuck a needle into my pelvic bone on the left side just above the buttock. I stared at the wall and concentrated as he counted to 10.

After he finished, he helped me pull up my pants and sit up. It had hurt, but pain without fear is far easier to handle. "Your bone marrow looks clean. But you will probably get chemotherapy," he said after examining the results. I nodded but

Dr. Barnes (My Oncologist)
Oil on canvas. 1991. 14" x 22"

could not manage to follow all he said after that. I was beginning to fade. "There is fluid around your heart. You will need to see another doctor." He looked at me carefully and said, "I will go to your mother and explain it all to her, too." Lydia came in to keep me company while I watched them talk.

We returned to my room so I could change into hospital pajamas, a gown that fastened in the back and baggy pants that fastened in the front. I was placed in the observation room, where I lay on a bed as the nurses searched for their IV special-ist. I was dehydrating fast and sensed their fear of the situation.

A tall, well-built man, in his thirties and wearing a moustache, approached me. "Hello, I am Dr. Leonard and I've come to help you feel better." A warm smile spread across his face as he looked down at me. "I am going to drain off some of the fluid around your heart to ease the pressure on it." He turned to a nurse and took the IV needle from her, saying, "Here, I can insert that." I felt a prick in my left hand, and the liquid traveled into my thirsty body. He sat down on my bed and continued to focus on me. "I heard you are an artist. When this is over, will you paint a picture for me?"

"Yes, I would love to," I replied weakly. I was pleased that somebody had told him I was an artist—my identity.

"Did you see the fauve exhibit at the Metropolitan Museum?" I nodded and said, "I loved it." He looked over to the other side of my bed, where they had wheeled in a stretcher. "Now I am going to help you onto this stretcher and we will go to presurgery in the main hospital." He gently lifted me onto the stretcher. Off we went down a maze of corridors, turning this way and that with a nurse and my mother following, like some bizarre procession.

As I lay there, I looked up at him pulling the stretcher along; he seemed reas-suring and protective. Here was somebody fighting with me. But then I looked into myself and saw darkness closing in all around. This time I was going all the way down, hitting bottom, and nothing could stop me.

We entered presurgery, where I was placed in a bed by the window. A man lay on my left, separated by hospital curtains; another man faced him. An old woman facing me stared at us with curiosity. The place smelled of dread.

Dr. Leonard lifted my gown and began to cleanse my chest, explaining everything as he did it. "I will give you some local anesthetic to numb the area so you won't feel anything." A happy, grinning young fellow, "Dr. Happy Face," appeared on my left with an echocardiogram (an instrument that records the heartbeat) to monitor the procedure on a computer screen. He chatted away as he pressed the electric eye to my flesh, just under my left breast. I focused on this discomfort to distract myself from the pain of the needles Dr. Leonard had inserted. Numbness spread across my chest.

Dr. Leonard (My Surgeon)
Oil on canvas. 1991. 14" x 22"

While Dr. Leonard began to drain the fluid, I lay very still and took in my surroundings. On my left, Dr. Happy Face continued to talk, thrilled over what he saw on the computer screen. Further down, at the foot of my bed, stood six or seven people, nurses and interns, all staring at my exposed chest, some open-mouthed. I caught a glimpse of Dr. Barnes in the far corner, watching with an expression of satisfaction, and then he was gone.

I averted my eyes from the crowd and looked at Dr. Leonard. For a young man he sure had a lot of gray hair. "You are such a good patient!" he exclaimed when he noticed my eyes on him. Fearing I might distract him, I shifted my focus to watch his hands and the tubes filling up with red-brown muck. After the fourth tube he stopped. "There, that should help you some." He smiled at me and dressed the wound.

I slept little that night, listening to the old woman across from me moan and watching the numbers on the blood pressure monitor go up and down while the strap across my arm squeezed and released continuously.

*E*arly the next morning the old woman was wheeled out for surgery. She screamed hysterically, "I am going to die! I won't survive this operation!" as she hung halfway out of the stretcher. It was so horrible to witness such naked fear that I blocked her from my mind.

Dr. Douglas walked in shortly afterward, smiling at me as he came over and sat down on my bed. I felt reassured by his presence.

"Darcy, they will have to perform another biopsy, just a small incision under your collar bone. Dr. Leonard will do it. We still don't know what type of lymphoma you have," he told me.

"Fine, the sooner the better—then I can get treatment," I said. I was relieved that Dr. Leonard would do the surgery. No mention had been made of Dr. Loblolly, and I was certainly not going to mention him.

At 6:00 PM, a stretcher was brought in for me. I removed everything except the hospital gown and climbed onto it. I turned and waved goodbye to my mother, who had spent the whole day with me. As I expected to see her after surgery, I said, "See you real soon."

I was wheeled into the hallway of the operating room, and a nurse put a hairnet on my head. After a few minutes she wheeled me into the room, where she and another nurse assisted me onto the operating table. The anesthetist inserted a needle into my left arm. "Let me know if anything feels wrong," she said.

As I became groggy they attached other things to me, which I could not identify. I heard Dr. Leonard speak over my head. "Okay Darcy, we will be done real soon." I looked up and saw only his eyes, then I went under *[PLATE 1]*.

ntensive Care ∽ I awoke in intensive care to see the anesthetist and Dr. Leonard peering into my face, their heads close to mine. I felt thirsty and groggy. Who was that man? Oh yes, Dr. Leonard. I tried to pull myself toward reality. A flash of pain and anger surged within me as I recognized him. Why had he hurt me?

The anesthetist smiled at me. "You're awake—we have you back." She pointed to the window, where I saw blankets and pillows on the ledge. "I spent most of the night here with you." I looked at her and blacked out.

Pieta / Start of the Climb
[Plate 1, page 93]
Oil on canvas. June 1991. 24" x 18"

When I opened my eyes I saw Dr. Douglas' face close to mine, and I began to cry. He put a hand on my shoulder, saying, "There, there, it's all right." A beeping sound went off and I realized I had a tube down my throat and another up my nose. "Oh, we'd better stop," said Dr. Douglas. I stopped crying and the beeping ceased.

An intern came up with a graph pad and a tiny pencil. I wrote, "Can I stay here?" Before I was admitted to the hospital, there had been talk of my going to a hospital in New Jersey for treatment.

"Yes, of course, everything will be taken care of," Dr. Douglas replied, and I dozed off.

I awoke to see my father holding my hand, and then I closed my eyes. I reopened them to see my mother holding my other hand. I thought how corny this must look: sickly daughter holding divorced parents' hands. Cilla then took my father's place. I saw her worried face and squeezed her hand to let her know "I am here," and I dozed off once more.

I reawakened and saw Dr. Barnes at the foot of my bed, smiling. " . . . and you are getting it right now!" was all I heard him say. I looked up at the side of my bed and saw an IV bag hanging from a rack. "Chemo. I am getting chemotherapy," I said to myself, and out I went again.

Finally, I became sufficiently aware to take in my situation. I was on a respirator, which explained the tubes in my nose and throat and the beeping noise. But there were other things in me as well: three IVs, one in the left side of my neck and bandaged up like a lopsided bullfrog, another in my left arm (which had swollen to twice its size), and the last in my groin, also the left side. A chest tube was in the pleural cavity by my left lung, the lower rib cage area (to drain out the lymphoma muck). The box at the end of it made bubbling sounds and looked like a child's ant farm, except it was full of liquid. A catheter was inserted into my bladder, a blood pressure strap around my right arm was continuously squeezing as before, and tied to a ribbon around my neck was a little box with three small suction cups attached to my flesh, near my heart. I dubbed it my "heart box."

I felt a strange numbness under my left breast; it was the incision Dr. Leonard performed for the biopsy. Why it was there, instead of below my collar bone, I did not understand. All I knew was that the incision, staples, stitches, and bandage felt as one.

So why did I feel so good? I could breathe, and there was no more pressure. An incredible sense of newness spread through me. I was completely exposed inside and out, and I was alive. It wasn't exactly a bed of roses, however. For one thing, I could not move (except my legs, to the envy of the rest of my body), and the intern had to periodically clean out the bag at the end of the tube down my throat, to make sure there was no build-up of any sort. He was sweet about it, apologizing each time he had to perform this dreadful task. The discomfort made my eyes tear, and I was required to cough, which was painful although he was gentle. He was a young, good-looking man with dark, curly hair and glasses, always with an expression of empathy on his face.

Between him and the nurses I felt protected and sheltered from any dangers. They gave me strength and comfort—the firm but soothing touch of a nurse encouraged my body to respond to the will to live. Two of the nurses I remember with fondness are Christine, a maternal young lady, and Carl, a most gentle young man. Both sensed my need for affection and warmth and responded in kind. I felt safe in their care.

Night came. I was given an injection of morphine and Valium so I could sleep. The head nurse, Thor, administered it. He was a big, blond Swede, who was brusque and efficient. "Here, I give you injection in your left thigh," he said as he turned me on my side to jab my leg.

The injection worked, and I awoke the next morning, completely unaware of the night hours having passed.

I wanted to see if I could still draw, and gripping the little pencil, I drew a potted plant that I saw on the counter of the nurse's station. Sitting precariously near the edge, it reminded me of a Matisse painting. Yes, I still had the ability.

Christine came in with bits of crushed ice. "You've been so good that I am going to let you have this. But don't swallow it. Keep it under your tongue." I stuck a piece in my mouth and sucked on it. The cool liquid was sumptuous.

I wanted to see if I could still draw, and gripping the little pencil, I drew a potted plant that I saw on the counter of the nurse's station.

I hated the tubes in my nose and throat and constantly wrote notes to the intern and Dr. Douglas asking when I would get them out. Finally, the intern got the okay from Dr. Leonard. He removed the tube from my throat first and then the one from my nose. He placed an oxygen mask on me. I closed my tear-filled eyes with relief and happiness, and my mind drifted.

"Heaven, I'm in heaven," I sang in my head. I was underwater, swimming with two large purple seals on either side of me [PLATES 2 AND 3]. We swam straight, not surfacing, and their big velvety black eyes looked into mine as we journeyed through the deep. I saw bright, emerald-green light above and rich, ultramarine darkness ahead while my protective seals stayed close by. To my disappointment, the intern switched my mask to a tube fitting comfortably into my nostrils, but when I closed my eyes the seals were still there.

Well, reality was waiting, so I kept my eyes open and spoke to my mother and sisters Amy, Cilla, and Lydia. My throat emitted a deep, gravelly sound and I grew hoarse quickly from the excitement and freedom to talk.

Seals I
[Plate 2, page 94]
Oil on canvas. June 1991. 28" x 16"

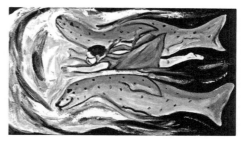

Seals II
[Plate 3, page 95]
Oil on canvas. July 1991. 28" x 16"

Night came again, and Thor administered another injection of Valium and morphine.

At daylight, Dr. Barnes quietly came in, and to my surprise and pleasure sat down on my bed and smiled tenderly at me. "I had to make a guess about your lymphoma. I didn't want to wait any longer for the test results before I gave you chemo, as you were in such danger." He spoke proudly but softly. He had made the right guess, and my tumor had shrunk dramatically after the first administration of chemo. He had saved my life.

Casey came in later, wearing a surgical mask to prevent giving me germs from a cold he had. He had flown in the night before from Seattle. We held hands and spoke of his dog Ringo and the drive they would make across the country.

Later in the morning the catheter was removed from my bladder, along with the IV in my groin. I graduated to the commode—such autonomy! I was sent off for chest x-rays. Piled into a wheelchair with chest tube and IVs, I was wheeled down to the x-ray room.

On my return to intensive care, Christine informed me that they would be moving me to a single room, as my bed was needed. Still piled with my paraphernalia in the wheelchair, I waved goodbye to my nurses and intern and off I went. I had been in intensive care for three days.

I settled in for the night with the help of a nurse and my mother (who promised to bring me some panties the next day, as all I had on was the hospital gown). I lay back in the dark and quiet, which was exhilarating and frightening at the same time. I slept deeply that night.

*R**emainder of My Stay in the Hospital* ∾ The anesthetist came into my room that morning. "How are you feeling now?" she asked. She sat on my bed and stared questioningly into my eyes. "We thought we'd lost you for a moment there." I felt alarmed but suppressed any thoughts that tried to surface, preferring to believe she'd just come for a visit. In fact, she had come to reassure herself that I was out of danger. When she left I began to wonder: what had actually happened to me in the operating room?

Dr. Leonard came in next to check my incision, so I gathered my courage and asked him."Well, you began to turn blue and told me you could not breathe, so I stuck a tube down your throat to see if there was any blockage," he told me matter-of-factly. "I couldn't see anything, so I performed the biopsy—it won't show under your breast—and put you on the respirator."

As I took all this in, a vague memory of not breathing came back to me and I brushed it aside. I thought about the incision: there must have been an awful lot of lymphoma muck for him to draw out, as it was a very large incision. I was afraid to ask, but I know that he too saved my life. The anesthetic must have added to the danger of the growing pressure of the tumor on my heart and lungs. Hence the dreadful fright for the anesthetist, who so carefully watched over me that night. She was a dedicated woman, and I felt lucky in my care at this hospital.

The incision became Dr. Leonard's concern. He took care of it, and I tried not to look but certainly felt it. The bullfrog IV in my neck was removed later that day and only the chest tube, heart box, and IV in my arm remained (the IV was changed to a new vein every three days). I was a bit more mobile now.

I was moved again, to a double room—the single one was needed for an AIDS patient. This time they moved me bed and all. My roommate Mary had the window side, while I was by the door and bathroom. Mary, not much older than me, was quite ill too. She was a tiny delicate lady, very gracious and brave. Our room filled with visitors every day, for we both had supportive families.

We were divided by a large, ugly, black and orange striped curtain, and the wall behind our heads was painted the same ugly orange. Luckily, we didn't have to stare at it, whereas our visitors had no choice. The other walls were painted a shade of off-white or pale blue. Across from me on the wall was a rubber-glove dispenser and a dreadful print of flowers in a vase. The only time I enjoyed looking at it was in the morning when the first rays of sunlight hit the wall. I'd squint my eyes and tilt my head, and behold, it became a seascape.

On my left was a bed table with a tissue box, sterilizing solutions, iodine, and dressing, which Dr. Leonard used to tend to my incision. Next to it was a tray table on wheels, where my meals were placed, along with many little belongings: tapes, a hand-made card from my friend Kevin (a fellow artist), a rock that my mother brought because it reminded us of Casey's sculpture, a book (a Tony Hillerman mystery), and a water pitcher—my world.

Next to the tray table was my commode. A guest chair was placed in the far corner on the other side of the entrance, which had two closets for patients. The bathroom was opposite these, on my immediate left. I looked forward to the day I could use it, confined as I was to the chest tube. The total size of the room was perhaps 10 by 16 feet.

*I*t was April 20, Casey's birthday, and all my family came to visit: Casey, all my sisters (Amy, Cilla, Emily, and Lydia), Lydia's husband Alun, my father and his wife, and of course my mother, who spent almost all of every day with me. I had a peaceful weekend and didn't miss my doctors' visits. I felt a strong urge to shield my family, as if the lymphoma might strike them. I was relieved that I had it instead of any of them. Casey had to leave on the next day, Sunday—the sooner he went, the sooner he'd be back. Saying goodbye again was painful for us both.

I reflected on my doctors' visits, which were important to me; by now I had figured out their schedules and knew when to expect each one. Dr. Leonard or Dr. Douglas came first thing in the morning, between 9:00 and 10:00 AM. Dr. Leonard would check my incision, change the dressing, and listen to my heart and lungs. He always retied the back of my gown afterward. He often sat on my bed, and we talked about my art as well as my health.

I treasured Dr. Douglas' visits. He came in every morning with a big smile on his face, never wearing a doctor's lab coat. He too listened to my heart and lungs, and then we would speak of my progress, the next steps in my treatment, and any questions I had, no matter how trivial. I had learned the hard way never to keep anything back again. He sat on my bed or the guest chair, and we would talk about my art or some family stories (like Casey's drive), as he was also the physician of my brother, sisters, and mother. I promised to show him and Dr. Leonard photos of my work.

Dr. Barnes arrived in the late morning or afternoon, often with a young intern in tow. The intern was an attractive woman from India, and she was extremely serious. Sometimes they would hold conference, one on either side of my bed, and I sat watching them as if watching a tennis match. If I was in a good mood I found it amusing; if I wasn't I found it irritating. I wanted to shout out "Hey, you two, I'm right here!"

Dr. Barnes examined me, always with an intense, focused expression on his face, listening to my heart and lungs and checking my lymph nodes for any swelling. I tried to converse with him then, and if I got him to smile I was pleased. It did not occur to me that he wore such a serious face to handle the enormous pressure of his job and all he had to be alert to in caring for cancer patients. All I wanted was for him to communicate with me. We spoke of my art only once or twice and I often felt he kept himself emotionally distant from me, but I never doubted his judgment or care.

I felt like a new child-woman. I saw myself sitting in my hospital bed with my arms open, wanting to be loved by the world. Something had happened to me in the operating room, releasing all my deepest desires and feelings and reaffirming my beliefs about life and art. For me, the world had changed.

Nighttime in the hospital was completely different from the daytime. Constant interruptions for blood pressure and temperature readings, medications, or tending to the needs of Mary or myself prevented any normal sleep. I was lucky if I totaled five interrupted hours of sleep a night. Add to this my being on prednisone (a steroid that is a real upper) around the clock, which made it even harder to sleep.

I noted that one other event always seemed to happen at night: death. Three people died while I was in the hospital. I only heard sounds, though; I did not see death. The first death was that of a man who groaned in agony for two nights in a row, then ceased the second night. The second death was also that of a man, but I did not hear him. What I did hear was his old mother wailing all night long until he died. I found out the next morning that she had been a tiny, old lady from a small town in Italy, dressed all in black. As was the custom in her culture, she held a lamentation for him until his demise. He was in his fifties and died of cancer. The last death was that of a woman. Her female companions paced up and down the hall crying, one louder than the other. I imagined them both in hats with flowers, one tall, the other short, comforting each other as well as they could.

Sometimes, when incidents like these happened, the nurses would rush into our room for reassurance. Our youth and the promise of recovery made them feel there was something to hope for. We were nicknamed the "pediatric ward."

The worst things also happened to me at night. The first incident was when my chest tube fell out. It had been in for almost a week, and one morning around 3:00 AM it came out. I had turned slightly in bed and felt a tug at my left side, followed by a warm wetness soaking my gown. I sat up in a panic, tried to hold the tube in place, and rang for the nurse. I shouted to someone out in the hall. Three or four nurses rushed in and removed the chest tube, for it had come out completely. They hurriedly bandaged the area with a huge bulky dressing and just as quickly they all vanished. I sat up in my bed, feeling abandoned and scared.

An intern was sent for; he came in briefly, examined me with self-importance, and left. He seemed unconcerned. My lung had not collapsed, so what was all the fuss? A technician came in after him to take x-rays, and he was very calm and sweet. He warned me about the coldness of the plate and reassured me with his smile and gentle manner. I was able to get a grip on myself and grab some sleep.

Later that morning I sat up, still wearing the same soaked gown, when Dr. Leonard came in. "Boy, am I glad to see you!" I blurted out. "Did you hear what happened? My chest tube fell out!"

"Let's see." He removed the bulky dressing. "It looks fine. I'll just put a fresh dressing on it," he said calmly. He replaced it with a smaller, snug-fitting bandage and redressed my incision. "Your body just rejected the tube—that's good." He smiled down at me placidly and left. I felt a little better but was still confused. Dr. Leonard's unsurprised attitude did not totally reassure me. At least a clean gown was brought in so that I could change.

Fortunately Dr. Douglas came in next, and after hearing my story he sat down on my bed, held my hand, and explained why it was good news. "Your body is getting stronger, Darcy. By rejecting the tube you show how well you are doing." It seemed very quiet—no more bubble sounds.

That evening Julia, my best friend, came to visit *[PLATE 13]*. I was glad she did not have to see me with the chest tube—pride, I suppose. It was dinner time, and as I could now move about on my own, I sat in the guest chair while Julia sat on the corner of my bed and talked to me. To our surprise, Dr. Loblolly walked in. "No one told me what happened! I was never notified of your situation." His tone was of hurt and mistrust. He moved between Julia and me, his red suspenders and bow tie standing out from his massive chest as he loomed over me. I smiled ironically and thought to myself how glad I was that nobody had told him. "Yes, well, here I am," I replied.

To save himself from increasing embarrassment and discomfort, he repeated a story of two sisters who were his patients: both had lymphoma at the same age, and both now had children and were fine. I smiled politely this time, hoping he would

Friends Triptych—Julia
[Plate 13, page 105]
Oil on canvas. August 1991.
14" x 20"

leave. When he finally did go (ran out of things to say) Julia and I looked at each other and burst out laughing, mostly from relief.

Later, after Julia had left, I was sent down for chest x-rays. I felt quite tired and my eyes had grown weak from the fluorescent lighting. Sunk down in my wheelchair, I waited for my escort to wheel me back to my room. Suddenly, I thought I saw death pass by. I rubbed my eyes and looked again. To my relief, it was only the resident rabbi *[PLATE 4]* walking down the hallway.

That night I had a hospital nightmare. Dr. Loblolly was chasing me down a dark corridor on a wheeled platform with a manic grin on his face and his grotesquely long arms hanging frozen at his sides *[PLATE 5]*. He shouted, "I will catch you and operate on you!" A huge contraption like a medieval torture device was behind him on the platform. "I always get the young women!" he continued to shout. I raced down the dark corridor, dressed only in my hospital gown. To my left were small cubicles with AIDS patients in them being tended by interns and on my right a wall of metal lockers (for bodies?). I started to cry, "Dr. Douglas, Dr. Douglas, help me!" I turned a corner and saw Dr. Douglas, with the same concerned expression he had when Dr. Loblolly was draining my lung. He shouted, "Here I am Darcy!" I awoke, worried that I had yelled his name aloud.

The Illusion in the X-Ray Room
[Plate 4, page 96]
Oil on canvas. Sept 1991. 16" x 22"

The Hospital Nightmare
[Plate 5, page 97]
Oil on canvas. July 1991. 16" x 24"

A week had now passed since the first half of my first chemotherapy treatment. It was now time for the second half. There were to be a total of six treatments, all in two parts. Except for slight nausea and vomiting, I felt pretty good and began to draw in a sketch book that Amy had brought me. She also brought some photos of my paintings so I could show them to Dr. Douglas and Dr. Leonard.

Both doctors loved my work and were amazed that I was really talented. I was pleased. I asked them if I could paint their portraits and mentioned that I also wanted to paint Dr. Barnes. They were eager and agreed. Dr. Leonard said, "We will be The Three Musketeers!" and he gestured with an imaginary sword, "One for all and all for one!" *[PLATE 17]*.

I started to run a fever the next day. Dr. Barnes came in to see me first. Putting a hand on my forehead, he said to the intern, "We can't release her yet—not with a fever!" I sat there with his hand on my head, feeling rather confused and thinking perhaps I goofed somehow, to have a fever. He looked at me and said, "You are having a reaction to the chemo. We will have to see if it develops further." He examined me in silence, then left.

Night came and I felt odd, slightly anxious and scared. At 2:00 AM another self-important young intern walked in, took the dressing off my incision, and pro-

The Three Musketeers
[Plate 17, page 109]
Oil on canvas. Sept 1991. 24" x 18"

nounced, "You have an infection in your incision, around the staples. We will have to remove them." He left abruptly, leaving me lying in bed with my gown drawn up and supporting my left breast with my hand.

I waited; no one came in and panic took hold of me. I began to worry about the infection: was it serious? Why hadn't Dr. Leonard come in that day to check it as he always had? I now felt scared and alone, and an uncontrollable terror like I had never felt before took hold of my soul. I tried to focus on something and my eyes caught Kevin's card, two beautiful abstract images of purity, color, light, beauty, and life. I wanted to lose myself in his painting, in something I believed in—art. It was the closest I came to praying to art; art was my religion.

A nurse finally came in. She sterilized and redressed my incision. I tried to keep her talking, of anything at all, just to keep myself calm. By morning I had so little control that I rang my mother as soon as I knew she would be up, and I began to cry on the phone. She hurried to catch the first train in from New Jersey. Next I rang Julia at work. Hearing her soothing voice kept the tears at bay for a while. I hung up when Dr. Douglas came in, and the flood gates opened. I couldn't stop the tears from pouring down my face.

Dr. Douglas quickly drew the curtains around my bed and said, "Darcy, you are having a reaction—it's okay." He spoke soothingly and put one hand on my shoulder and the other on my knee as I sat cross-legged in my bed. "It is a reaction to the chemo. You will probably run a fever of 102° by evening before it goes down. It is all right."

"I'm sorry, I can't seem to stop crying." I sobbed through my tears, curled up into myself.

"If you didn't cry we would worry," he said reassuringly as he looked into my face and continued to hold me. But it was hard to listen because I was beginning to feel paranoia. He continued to repeat words of comfort, emphasizing what was happening to me, when Dr. Leonard walked in.

I was a bit embarrassed, crying in front of two of my doctors, but it was unavoidable. Dr. Douglas spoke a few words to Dr. Leonard and quietly left. Dr.

Leonard came up to me and said, "Darcy, what is the matter?" with a look of real concern on his face.

"I'm afraid," I replied, still crying. I wanted to say I was afraid of everything but could not get the words out.

"We are going to remove the staples and stitches today. You have an infection in your incision," he said, smiling sweetly at me. "My assistant will do it. You'll like her—she is a real nice lady." He checked the dressing on my incision.

"Will it hurt?" I asked, knowing full well I wasn't afraid of the pain. What I was afraid of I could not begin to define.

"You won't feel anything." He put out his hand for me. "You'll be fine." He stood holding my hand and continued to smile warmly at me. "Cheer up. You're okay!" He gave me the thumbs-up sign as he went out the door.

At midday the fear subsided. Later in the afternoon, the stitches and staples were removed and I was told I could have a shower. It was the only shower I had in the hospital, and it was such a luxury to feel really clean. Amy helped me, holding my hand or arm to make sure I did not slip or get the incision too wet. My normal wash routine was to use the sink in the bathroom, sticking in one foot at a time while holding onto the towel rack, which also balanced my heart box. I washed everywhere I could, except for most of my chest.

*L*ife had improved since the reaction: Dr. Barnes cut down my prednisone and started me on a course of IV antibiotics, which I took day and night. He also gave me special shots of Neupogen to boost my white blood count (WBC), which had dropped drastically. My body seemed to have a lot of ups and downs. Dr. Douglas explained to me that I had a dramatic body—it reacted in extremes. "Just like my personality!" I responded.

My face and left arm, which had been swollen from medications, were now back to normal. I finally recognized that woman in the mirror; I had myself back. My family hugged and kissed me now, especially since the day Julia climbed into my bed.

This so delighted Lydia that she did it the next day. I loved it—a beautiful way to say, "I am not afraid to come into the illness with you." It was very lonely in there sometimes.

Lydia and Alun had found an apartment for my mother and me in Brooklyn, close enough to the hospital. My father would cover the rent while my mother (lucky her) would be my "nurse." We would move into it in the middle of May. In the meantime, we'd stay with Amy in her apartment on the Upper West Side of Manhattan—that is, if I ever got out; it had already been more than two weeks.

My heart box had been removed, and all I wore now was the IV needle. I could toss and turn all I wanted to. Fran, another very dear friend, came for a visit and we took a walk to the waiting room *[PLATE 13]*. I held onto her arm and shuffled along. My torso felt like a block of ice, whereas my legs just wanted to move. It was hard to keep harmony among the body parts. As we sat together talking about nothing in particular, my eyes were overwhelmed by all there was to see. Just to look out the window at the city was amazing. Fran helped me back to my room before she left, and again it was such a strange sensation to walk.

Dr. Leonard came in soon afterward and solemnly informed me that I was to be in for a few more days. He wanted to be sure my infection had cleared up completely. I was so tired and exhausted from lack of sleep and hospital life that I wanted to scream at him. Instead I just sat in my bed and glared, saying nothing. He gave up after a minute or two and went out to my mother in the hall and asked her to explain why I had to stay, but she knew better and said nothing. Worst of all, Mary was getting out. Although I was happy for her, I felt left behind and would miss her. She had been a comfort to me the day I had the reaction, telling me that the intern had no right to scare me, that he was just showing off, and that I should pay no attention to him. It was

Friends Triptych—Fran
[Plate 13, page 105]
Oil on canvas. August 1991. 14" x 20"

the first time we really talked, and I found out she had been fighting a difficult illness for some time. I admired her spirit.

That night, while listening to Debussy on my Walkman and watching the antibiotic drip into my veins, I had a vision of myself in a garden, alone among broken statues in a gray haze. My head was bald (my hair was already falling out from chemo) and I was as still as a statue. I was in limbo, a place of isolation *[PLATE 6]*. I had a solitary ordeal ahead of me.

Music was such a comfort to me and a wonderful way to escape from everything. Casey made a tape for me of Van Morrison's album *Enlightenment,* which I played over and over. The words and music fit so well with my emotions, and his voice was soothing and reassuring. I loved to listen to him most when the first rays of sunlight hit the wall opposite me and a soft golden glow filled the room with hope.

*T*he three-week mark of my stay was fast approaching. Dr. Douglas marched in one morning and threw his hands up in the air. "I've just been arguing with your doctors to let you go home, but they won't let me release you until Friday!" He sat down on my bed and smiled, saying, "I'm sorry Darcy, I've tried everything I could think of." He took my hand.

In the Garden
[Plate 6, page 98]
Oil on canvas. June 1991. 24" x 18"

"That's okay. You tried." I had managed to obtain some sleep the night before, and as it was already Wednesday I wasn't too bothered. "So maybe you'll have to break me out of this joint," I joked. (I had visions of Dr. Douglas sneaking me out in a doctor's lab coat or escaping off the roof of the hospital in a helicopter.) I told him of these two plans, which he laughingly agreed with because he understood my love of visual jokes.

Just then Dr. Leonard walked in with a frown on his normally cheerful face. He avoided looking at Dr. Douglas and spoke in a grumpy tone to me. "Darcy, let's

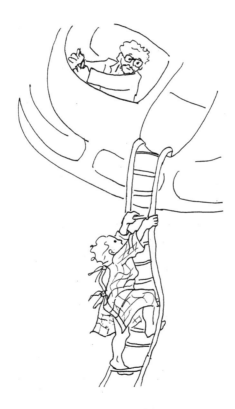

I had visions of Dr. Douglas sneaking me out in a doctor's lab coat or escaping off the roof of the hospital in a helicopter.

see how your incision is doing." I assumed the usual position of lying on my back, holding my left breast up so he could squeeze out any pus from the infection. As I lay there, Dr. Douglas rubbed my feet and said, smiling, "He can worry about your incision, but I'm not worried." An expression of pain crossed his face, as he knew all this squeezing hurt. After several minutes he stopped rubbing my feet and said, "I'll see you tomorrow, Darcy." We grinned broadly at each other before he left.

Meanwhile Dr. Leonard was still squeezing away with a frown on his face. I suddenly flinched in pain and his expression softened. "Sorry, Darcy, I know it hurts, but I want to get out all the pus I can."

"That's okay." Not only did this incision hurt, but so did my right hand, which he grasped in the process of squeezing, because my IV needle was in it. I said nothing, oddly enough, for I found it funny, just as I did my doctors disagreeing; it was the only time I ever saw them do so.

The day before my release, Dr. Barnes came in early to see me because he had to leave town for a few days. He sat on my bed, only the second time he did so, and after he examined me we spoke about the chemotherapy. I would receive treatments in his office, located in the hospital complex. I showed him some photos of my work and asked if I could paint him. Pleased but shy, he agreed. We spoke some more about chemo, which I felt was pretty tolerable, but to my surprise he reacted oddly. He stood up and said, "If you think this is manageable, wait until you have a bone marrow transplant!" I looked questioningly at him. "You'll be so full of drugs—really sick. You won't thank me then." (I had thanked him earlier for saving my life.) He abruptly left.

I sat in my bed confused, scared, and hurt. What had I said? Why a transplant? Had I crossed a line with him? Dr. Douglas came in to find me in this emotional muddle. "What's the matter, Darcy?" he asked and quickly came over and sat by me. I told him what had passed between Dr. Barnes and me; after 20 minutes of hand-holding and explaining why I probably would not need a bone marrow transplant—I was responding so well to this chemo—I cheered up.

*T*he next morning I got up and dressed in clothes. It was the day of my release. Dr. Leonard came in one last time to dress my incision, and we set up a date for an appointment at his office, also in the hospital complex. Dr. Douglas came in next, and after he reviewed everything with me I gave him a long speech about what a wonderful doctor and friend he was. He modestly thanked me and we hugged each other. After he left my mother came in. I hugged my nurse Rhonda, a favorite of mine, and off we went.

Alun picked us up, and as we drove away my senses were overtaken by all the colors, smells, and sounds. It was now early May.

2

Intermission: Adjusting to My New Life

The next few weeks were a period of recuperation and learning. I was regaining my strength, finding out what damage had been done to my body, and learning about the medications I would take in conjunction with chemotherapy. There were good things: Casey returned for good with his now big puppy, Ringo. I enjoyed the nearby park every day—the colors of nature still amazed my eyes. I ate, slept, and drew.

My first problem was losing my hair. Already I had lost clumps and was disgusted each time I washed my hair. I knew I had to do something about it. My skin had become sensitive from chemotherapy, so I was too nervous to shave my head. Instead, I cut my hair—the saying "If it offends you, cut it off" came to mind as I clipped away. I did not stop until I had only "peach fuzz," about a quarter inch of hair. In some places I had bald patches.

My first reaction to my new look was that my eyes seemed to have grown to twice their size, and my head appeared totally defenseless. As I ran my hands along my scalp, my skull felt reassuring. I turned my head left and right, trying to adjust to my new look. All I saw was vulnerability, no place to hide—my face showed everything.

I needed to find some bald role models. Two performers sprang to mind: Sinead O'Connor, a beautiful, talented singer who was bald, and Patrick Stewart, an actor on the television show *Star Trek: The Next Generation*—I called him my "bald buddy." It helped me to feel less weird, less alone in my baldness.

Next I had the body to deal with, the incision first. A deep rose scar ran along the curve under my left breast. Because all the nerves had been cut during surgery, my side below the left breast and the breast, up to the nipple, were numb. I also had two smaller scars on my chest, one where the fluid had been drained near my heart and another where my chest tube had been inserted. Both held scabs that fell off early, leaving more rose-colored marks. My scars were the reminders of my battle with death, which I reflected on sadly but with pride.

I had two projects: eating and taking medications. I had lost the art of eating in the hospital, but it miraculously returned when I got out. I craved liquids (chemo dehydrates the body), required plenty of protein (chemo burns it up), and could eat as much as I wanted (chemo burns everything up). I usually ate five small meals a day. I loved fruits, fruit juices (except orange juice for some odd reason), salads, pasta, and ice cream (which was especially soothing on my battered throat). For protein, I ate chicken, tuna, turkey, eggs, or cheese. I disliked cooked vegetables, except for carrots. I drank no coffee or alcohol; for caffeine, I had only two weak cups of tea a day. Because I was always thirsty, I drank a lot of water.

For dessert I had a fine selection of medications: I took prednisone, my "upper," three times a day after meals, 12 days in a row, starting after the first half of each chemo treatment. For days on which I received chemo, I was excused from it. Compazine fought my nausea on chemo days. I took one before treatment and one four hours later as well as any other time I felt nauseated. Lorazepam was my "knock-out" pill, which I took as soon as I returned home after a chemo treatment, and for the 12 nights of prednisone, to help me sleep. Leucovorin was the magic pill I took exactly

24 hours after the second half of each chemo treatment, six times and six hours apart. I believe it was to help my body readjust. Hell, Dr. Barnes told me to take it, so I did. Sulfa tablets were my "horse pills" (see the Marx Brothers film, *A Day at the Races*) to prevent pneumonia, which I took 3 days a week, twice a day, with A LOT OF WATER (this is how it was printed on the bottle). With these, I used two over-the-counter drugs: an antacid, for the dreadful gas pains prednisone caused, and an antihistamine, which I used as an alternative to the knock-out pills.

Life was strange. I was still so weak that I found it hard to readjust. Walking about or just turning my torso was an effort at times; I felt as if my body might shatter. Eventually, however, I started to enjoy the semblance of a normal life.

*M*y first return to the hospital was for my checkup with Dr. Leonard. Just the thought of stepping into the building was frightening. As I waited in his examining room, I began to panic, and everything seemed to close in on me. Luckily, Dr. Leonard walked in wearing his unique grin, and I relaxed. "How are you doing, Darcy? You look great! Is it good to be out?"

"Thank you," I replied shyly, wearing a scarf to hide my baldness. "It is so nice to be able to sleep at night again."

"I don't know how anyone could sleep in a hospital," he responded to my complete surprise. It dawned on me that most doctors have no idea what it is like to be a patient in the hospital. He examined my scar. "It is doing fine. See me in 3 weeks." I went home, no longer afraid of the hospital.

My second chemo went fairly smoothly. I learned not to eat anything afterward, until the next day. I always vomited after each treatment, more so after the second half. I drank ginger ale to be sure I'd vomit up something—it was awful hacking up nothing. Dr. Barnes' nurse, Kate, gave me lots of tips on how to handle reactions to chemo. I learned to ask her many questions as time went on, and her advice was invaluable.

I later went to see Dr. Douglas for a checkup and showed him my bald head. His response boosted my ego: "You look like a fashion designer!" After examining me, he told me he would be away for 5 days, through the Memorial Day weekend.

We were now in our Brooklyn apartment. After my checkup with Dr. Douglas I had set up my easels and started to paint. I was happy and excited—then I started to feel hot. The next day my fever hit 101°. I rang Dr. Barnes, who instructed me to come to the hospital and to pack a small bag in case I had to stay in the clinic for a few days.

I sat in the examining room of his office, fighting back tears of frustration and fear. Dr. Barnes walked in and I began to cry, unable to contain them any longer. "Don't worry, Darcy. I can handle this," he said assuredly. "I'd be upset too, but it is probably just an infection. We will put you in the clinic for a few days on IV antibiotics." He reiterated, "This is something I can take care of." I still wept as I lay on the table so he could examine me. To comfort me he spoke of my art. "You could set up your easel in the clinic—start a clinic series!" Now it was Dr. Barnes' turn to make me smile.

There was only one minor problem: Dr. Douglas was away and Dr. Barnes would be away the next day, Friday. Who would see me on that day? Dr. Loblolly was called; he would come in and see me. "Oh well," I thought, "I'm sure he'll be fine." Cultures were ordered. This required my being stuck in the arm three times, to my great displeasure. I was so tired of being stuck with needles.

By evening my mother—my care partner—and I settled into our room; we had checked back into "Hotel Clinic."

3

In the Clinic, or
Three Weeks for Bad Behavior

Adventures with Dr. Loblolly ∾ I was now back in the clinic, only this time I was aware of my surroundings. The examination rooms, offices, and nurses' station were all on one floor; on the next floor, immediately above, was the cafeteria where we ate all our meals. The "hotel rooms" were the next five floors below. Our private room with bath was large and spacious; we had a television, a small refrigerator, two guest chairs, a coffee table, and comfortable beds—very nice accommodations, although given my situation, I was never able to appreciate them fully.

My first nurse, Iris, set up my antibiotic schedule and inserted an IV needle into my left hand. I wore a fish-net glove over it when not in use. My schedule was simple; at 10:00 every morning and 9:30 every night I was to be given antibiotics.

Friday passed quietly. Amy came at 6:00 in the evening with my requested items (sketchbook, Walkman), and we sat in the room talking, preparing to go up to dinner, when a phone call came from the nurses' station—Dr. Loblolly had arrived. We went upstairs and waited. He came out of the elevator wearing his red suspenders and a silly grin. I rose to greet him, holding my most recent chest x-rays.

He ushered me into an examining room, his arms waving about either side of me, frequently touching me.

As I sat on the examination table, Dr. Loblolly darted around me, preparing to listen to my lungs and heart. This furtive pawing about to listen to my organs so infuriated me that I flung up my shirt in defiance. I had worn no bra, as it would have irritated my scar, and he stepped back slightly before putting the stethoscope to my heart. I lowered my shirt while he looked at the x-rays. "These white spots may be the lymphoma returning," he told me.

"Where? How can you tell? Dr. Barnes believes it is an infection."

Once more his arms were around me as he eagerly showed me the x-rays. "See, here and here. No, I think it is the lymphoma returning." He sounded pleased. "I'll need to perform a bronchoscopy." He continued to flutter about me.

"But Dr. Leonard already did that," I responded quickly.

Dr. Loblolly walked over to the only chair and sat down. He turned to face me with a rather icy smile. "We are going to get to know each other real well. There has been too much interference. It is good I am back in the picture again." A smug look appeared on his face; abruptly he snapped, "Who did the biopsy?"

"Dr. Leonard did it, with Dr. Barnes overseeing the procedure." I was bewildered now. Where on earth was this guy coming from?

"Well, they did it all wrong! This Dr. Leonard didn't know what he was doing!" He sat silently, staring at the wall in front of him with a glazed look in his eyes. Doubts flew into my mind. Had I missed something? Could he be right? I spoke up, "Dr. Barnes was in charge. I know he isn't very talkative, but . . ."

"Dr. Barnes is very secretive—you can't get anything out of him!" retorted Dr. Loblolly, and he stood up and came toward me. Alarmed and feeling I had somehow betrayed Dr. Barnes with my words, I kept quiet. I was shocked that he had the gall to criticize my doctors to my face.

"I might stick a tube in your lung instead of down your throat—it would be much quicker. There is the danger that your lung might collapse, though," he pondered out loud.

I thought to myself, "Oh great! Talk about nightmares coming true." I decided to humor him and just get out of there. I was nothing more than a guinea pig to him. I eyed the door between him and me. "Okay, whatever you think is best. When do you think you will perform this operation?" I asked as nonchalantly as I could.

"As soon as possible. I need to review it with Dr. Barnes before I set a time." We went to my mother and Amy, and he informed them of his plans.

"Doesn't Dr. Douglas have a say in this?" asked my mother. "After all, he is her physician."

"No, no, dear lady. Dr. Douglas doesn't have any say at all—and get that look off your face." She was glaring at him in anger. "Only Dr. Barnes and I do." He dismissed the subject with a wave of his hand. "I must return to my office. They are wallpapering it. I hope they don't make a mess of it." He left and we stormed up to dinner. He had managed to insult all my doctors and my mother—I was furious.

We spent the weekend discussing it with the rest of our family and with Fran and Julia. All agreed with us that his behavior was atrocious. At night, I worried that Dr. Barnes would not return in time and that Dr. Loblolly would operate on me. I did not realize that I had the power to prevent him from doing so. I spoke with my nurse, Helen **[PLATE 14]**, about it. A wonderful, wise woman, she listened carefully to my story. "Tell Dr. Barnes about it. He'll take care of him. I've known Dr. Loblolly a long time, and I've never heard of such behavior from him . . . but you know what? I'm not surprised!"

Nurse Helen
[Plate 14, page 106]
Oil on canvas. August 1991. 16" x 20"

*O*n Monday morning Dr. Barnes came back. Smiling cheerfully, he found us an examining room. Once inside, I burst out with the events of Friday evening. His expression changed as I told him, "Dr. Loblolly said the lymphoma was returning and that I'd need a special operation. He was very aggressive and . . . "

"Aggressive!" he interrupted me. "He has no right to be aggressive!" He paced back and forth in the small space, his face now flushed with anger.

"Wait, let me finish. He also said that you and Dr. Leonard did the biopsy wrong, that Dr. Douglas has no say in the matter—and he was even rude to my mother!" I paused to catch my breath.

"Well, he is wrong." He spoke calmly but firmly now. "I am sure it is an infection. We will have the lab test results tomorrow."

"But he insulted my doctors to me! How could he do that?"

"I don't know what he is talking about." He waved one hand in the air. "The biopsy went very well." He avoided saying anything against Dr. Loblolly.

"I don't want him near me. I don't want him to touch me."

"Okay Darcy, he won't." He looked kindly at me now. "After this week he is out of the picture. I am 99% sure it is an infection and that you won't need an operation."

"Well, I just don't want to deal with him anymore."

"I promise. After this week, no more Dr. Loblolly." It was the first time I ever saw Dr. Barnes angry, and he was right: it was an infection. I never saw Dr. Loblolly again.

*M*ore Tests: The "Big Pill" ∿ I did not really feel better until that evening, when to my surprise and relief, Dr. Douglas was back. After examining me and listening to my adventure with Dr. Loblolly and all my fears, he comforted me, and I felt safe again. I also realized that this incident had broken barriers between Dr. Barnes and me.

My daily routine of antibiotics continued, and my IV needle was switched to another vein after three days, and again after three more. My arms quickly covered with bruises, and my left one swelled up once more. My infection was still undiagnosed, so a specialist was called in. He looked like Jose Ferrer, and although he was nice enough, I was sick of seeing more doctors. He decided that I needed some tests, and I was sent several times for echocardiograms. He was sure the infection was related to my heart. Nothing turned up, so he decided I needed another test— he was determined to prove his theory. "It's easy, Darcy. Just a big pill you have to swallow," Dr. Barnes and Dr. Douglas assured me. "It won't hurt."

I went for the test, my mother accompanying me. We waited and waited. The doctor who was to perform the procedure came out to review it with me. To my surprise, it was Dr. Happy Face. He didn't remember me, though. He explained the procedure to me. "We will be able to see down your esophagus this way," he concluded, smiling.

Dr. Douglas came down to find me and give me a little moral support. I was getting nervous about swallowing this pill—it didn't sound quite right to me. "It will be fine," he said as he stood by me. Dr. Happy Face was on my other side, bobbing his head and grinning away in agreement. I suppose it was one big adventure for him. He attempted to emulate Dr. Douglas and touched my shoulder, telling me not to worry.

Finally I was called in. I stripped to the waist and put on a hospital gown. I then lay down on the table on my left side, with my arm folded under my head and my knees bent. A towel was placed under my chin. Dr. Happy Face sat directly in front of me with the "pill." It was no pill, I can assure you, but a long tube with a camera eye at the end. I had to get this down my throat?

Dr. Happy Face sprayed local anesthetic down my throat and placed a plastic ring in my mouth for me to bite down on (instead of a silver bullet). He gingerly slid the tube down through the plastic ring, but I gagged and he had to withdraw it. "I'm sorry," I gasped. A nurse came round me and said, "Wait, let's try this." She had me bend more sharply at the waist and knees and tuck my head further down. "Okay, now try," she said.

Another doctor, with a rather daft expression, had joined us to observe the procedure. I did not like the looks of him at all. "She can get it down," he stated to everyone, and to me, "Just swallow it!" We decided to ignore him. Even Dr. Happy Face was annoyed by his colleague and actually frowned.

Once again the tube was put through the ring in my mouth, and this time it went down. I tried to keep calm, but an uncontrollable trembling took over my body. "Hold still, hold still!" shouted the daft-looking doctor. The nurse lay her hand on my waist and kept it there, saying, "You're okay. It's all right." She spoke soothingly and I stopped shaking.

"You are doing fine, just great!" said Dr. Happy Face and he pointed to the screen. "We can get an image now." They all crowded around the screen to look as I lay drooling profusely. After what seemed ages, Dr. Happy Face said, "Great—I see no sign of infection. It looks clear to me." He slowly withdrew the tube and I coughed. After helping me to get up, he told me, "You will have a bit of a sore throat for a day or two, but that is all." He beamed at me.

"Sorry I gagged the first time," I said, sitting dazed but relieved that it was all over.

"Oh no, that's perfectly normal. Most people take three or four tries before they can swallow it! You did great!" He grinned and bounced out happily.

Later that day I told Dr. Barnes about it. "How did you do it? It would have taken them all day to get it down my throat! I would never have swallowed it!" He looked at me in amazement. I boasted in reply, "Well, it wasn't so hard."

Later I found out that both Dr. Barnes and Dr. Douglas had felt bad that I had to take this test. They knew the infection wasn't related to my heart, but as they produced no other answer, the Jose Ferrer doctor had his way. I decided he wasn't so nice anymore.

"**M**r. Hickman" Enters My Life ∾ In the hospital, Dr. Barnes mentioned I might need a Hickman catheter at some point; when he saw the condition of my arms, he decided it had better be soon. Dr. Leonard would perform the operation, to my great relief. I didn't want another doctor taking a knife to me.

A Hickman catheter is a long tube inserted into a vein in the chest, just under the collarbone. It exits about 2½ inches lower (the tube runs under the skin), above the breast. The outer tube ranges in length and can have one to three heads (where IV medications are injected). Mine was roughly 16 inches long and had two heads.

As Dr. Barnes discussed the Hickman with me, he gave me a surprise. I was to be in the clinic for a total of three weeks. As I had an unidentified infection I would need 21 days of antibiotics. This was a standard procedure.

"What? Three weeks! I'll go nuts!" I yelled at him.

"Look at it this way, you are already on day 11, halfway through," he shouted back at me as he suppressed a smile.

"But I want to go home and paint. You've no idea what it's like being caught here. I can't stand it..." I shook my head.

"I know, I know," he said sympathetically. "Why don't you bring your easel and paints and set up in the clinic?"

"Sure!" I responded sarcastically. "I can't bring oil paints into a hospital. Can you imagine what people would say about the smell and the mess?" The argument continued, but of course Dr. Barnes won in the end. I furiously stormed back to my room, to find Amy, Cilla, Lydia, Alun, Emily, and my friend Donna waiting for me. It was Sunday, and they all sat chatting with my mother.

"Three weeks—a total of three weeks in here! I can't take it! I'll go stir crazy!" I yelled as I stormed in. Donna, whom I had not seen for some time, came up to hug me. She had not seen me bald or angry before. "Darcy, you look great, and it is wonderful to see you so angry!" she exclaimed as we hugged each other.

*T*he next day was Hickman day. I was scheduled for surgery at 3:00 PM and could not eat or drink anything after breakfast. The Jose Ferrer doctor decided I needed one more test to see if I had a clot in my left arm—he just wouldn't give up. The test was at 2:00 PM and ran late. It was simple, like the electrocardiogram—an electric eye pressed to the flesh. No clots were found, so I hurried back to the clinic, got into hospital pajamas (at least I could keep my panties on this time), and went to have Dr. Barnes and Nurse Helen check me out.

As I ran down the hall of the clinic, all the other patients' eyes were on me. I heard their thoughts as I raced by: "She's young, she's running and she's bald!" Nurse Helen approached me and placed an arm around my shoulders. "You look so cute!" she exclaimed and squeezed me as we walked into the examining room.

"The Sinead O'Connor look," I told her as we went inside, where Dr. Barnes was waiting for us. On seeing me bald he showed no great surprise beyond doing a double take (until that time I had worn a scarf to cover my head). Then he and Nurse Helen took my vital signs. "Doesn't she look like Sinead O'Connor?" she asked. "You're setting a trend, Darcy." She turned and grinned at me.

"Remember to tell Dr. Leonard to put the Hickman in your right side—just in case," said Dr. Barnes, nodding in reply to Nurse Helen's question. (Did he even know who Sinead O'Connor was?)

SHE'S YOUNG, SHE'S RUNNING, AND... SHE'S BALD!

As I ran down the hall of the clinic all the other patients' eyes were on me.

"Okay," I answered. "Do you have a crayon so I can draw an X or write 'Put Hickman here'?"

"How about this pen?" He pulled one from his pocket and we all laughed and left the examining room.

I sat in a wheelchair, waiting a long time for an escort to wheel me to the operating room. She finally showed up and, boy, was she a bad driver: we careened around corners and nearly crashed into walls—it would have been safer to walk. Luckily we didn't get a speeding ticket, and after we emerged from the OR elevator she went off duty. A pleasant young nurse approached me. "Hi, I'm Judy, and I'll be helping you today. Why did you arrive in a wheelchair?" she asked, finally noticing how I came. "Everyone comes in a stretcher."

"The big elevator in the clinic is broken, so here I am!"

"Okay, well this is certainly different." She wheeled me to an operating room, where another nurse was waiting for us. "Hey, you're early—Dr. Leonard isn't here yet," she told us. Then she smiled at me, saying, "Hi, my name is Melissa." They assisted me onto the operating table, shaped to fit the human body. Above I saw massive lights, and to my left above the entrance were two huge television sets. Lots of medical cabinets and other contraptions were about as well as things I could not identify.

I lay on the table with the hospital pants pulled down so they could affix a big pad on my right thigh. A blood pressure strap was fastened to my left arm, a cord was taped to my right index finger, my IV was hooked up, and a strap was fastened around my waist. We waited. I grew cold and Melissa placed two blankets on me. We joked to pass the time, and my sense of humor and good nature surprised them. It was only to keep myself calm, and they were awfully young. I wanted them to feel comfortable with the "patient."

At 4:30 PM Dr. Leonard came rushing in, apologizing profusely. "I'm sorry, Darcy, they just told me you were here. I've been waiting the whole time."

"We were both waiting!" I laughed to hide my anxiety.

"I'll just go scrub up and be right back." He rushed out, and I imagined him scrubbing up like the Marx Brothers in the doctor episode of *A Day at the Races.* Perhaps he would return wearing a lab coat with "Joe's Garage" printed on it.

He returned and donned a thick surgeon's apron over his blue doctor's uniform. He also wore a hairnet, goggles, and face mask, and of course rubber gloves. He looked like an alien or an astronaut. "Are you okay, Darcy? Do you want a mild sedative?" he asked behind his mask as he loomed over me and uncovered my chest in preparation. "It would just make you groggy."

Memories of my last experience in OR haunted me. "No, thank you, I'm fine—really."

"We can't find the radio," said Judy. "Melissa looked everywhere for it."

"I could sing," suggested Dr. Leonard. "But you all might run out screaming."

"Don't forget to put the Hickman in my right side," I said.

"Okay. Sure you don't want anything?" His eyes questioned me.

"Nah, I'm fine—just hungry."

I imagined Dr. Leonard scrubbing up like the Marx Brothers in the doctor episode of "A Day at the Races."

"Well, I just happen to have a pizza in my back pocket for afterward," he replied, his eyes smiling now.

"I hope you haven't squashed it."

"Nope!" He began to scrub my chest with different solutions, using a stick with a sponge at the end of it. "Okay, I'm just sterilizing your chest now," he explained and dunked the sponge into a large barrel full of liquid. I felt like a car in a car wash. "This is iodine," he continued. Judy started to build a tent around my head to prevent me from seeing and getting splattered. I heard Dr. Leonard's voice from behind it. "Now some local anesthetic to numb the area." I grew nervous as the needles were stuck into my chest. "Next I am placing a sheet of film over the whole area to keep it sterile. Do you want to see it?"

"Okay." I felt it necessary to communicate with him as much as possible, to remind him that I was there. But he did not forget.

"See, just a sheet of film." He laid it down on my chest. "Okay, we are ready. Let me know if you feel anything."

I fought to keep from trembling, and it began. I heard grinding sounds and felt light tugs and taps on my chest and collarbone. There were loud clinks of operating tools on the metal tray as he asked the nurses for this or that instrument. Suddenly I felt a sharp pain in my right breast. "Ow!" I yelled out.

"Sorry, Darcy, sorry!" He quickly administered more anesthetic to that area. "Sorry about that."

"That's okay," I said weakly. I knew I must be shaking a lot now. His body pressed into my right arm as the grinding sounds and tugs continued. Finally he finished, just in time. I was afraid I'd shake even more and interrupt the operation.

"Okay, just a couple of small stitches, Darcy, and then we are done." I visualized him with a long thread and needle, like a tailor mending away. "There, I'll just clean you up." Judy dismantled the tent around my head as Dr. Leonard cleansed my chest and bandaged the Hickman. He removed the goggles and face mask. I saw his face and relaxed.

"You okay?"

"Yeah, thanks," I replied and looked at the clock on the wall. The whole procedure had taken exactly 30 minutes.

"Do you remember anything from the last time you were here?" he asked quietly, an expression of empathy on his face as he stroked my arm.

"No." I looked up at him.

"Good." He smiled affectionately at me. "I'll just get out of the rest of this stuff."

Dr. Leonard left, and as I looked at the turned-out lights above me, I saw my reflection. I almost cried, but my artist's curiosity got the better of me, and I stared at my image. That bald, pale, semiclothed person was me. I seemed so fragile and vulnerable, totally defenseless in my battle *[PLATE 8]*.

After x-rays were taken Dr. Leonard gingerly helped me back into the hospital pajamas and off the operating table into my wheelchair. Once he got me seated, he proceeded to tuck the blankets around me as if for a baby, grinning at me like a protective big brother. I laughed and said, "Well, all I need now is a bottle, preferably one full of wine."

Dr. Leonard hopped onto the operating table while we waited for the x-rays and asked, "Can't you have a drink between chemos?"

"Yeah, but the thought of putting alcohol into me with all that medication is nauseating," I replied.

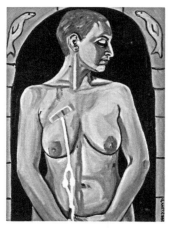

Self Portrait / Reflection
[Plate 8, page 100]
Oil on canvas. August 1991. 20" x 28"

"You are probably wise not to."

"When this is all over, I am going to become a drunken slut."

Dr. Leonard and Judy laughed, and he turned to her and said with pride in his voice, "Darcy is a painter and a really good one, too!" The x-ray was brought in. "Oh, here's the x-ray—let's see how I did." He hopped off the table to look at it on the light box. "Hmmm, pretty good job." He paused. "Sexy."

"Whatever turns you on," I said from under the blankets, and on the x-ray, I caught sight of the tube in me. Right now I did not feel sexy. I was exhausted and my good cheer was fading. Dr. Leonard wheeled me back to the elevators with Judy. They enjoyed my arriving in a wheelchair instead of a stretcher. Of course, I preferred to be sitting up instead of lying down, as I felt less vulnerable.

"If it hurts I can prescribe Tylenol with codeine for you," he said as we arrived at the OR elevators.

"I'm sure regular Tylenol will be fine." All I felt was a numbness in my right shoulder and collarbone, and I was starting to feel depressed.

Dr. Leonard left, only to return a minute later with a hairnet, which he put on my head. I adjusted it to a beret. He smiled tenderly at me and walked away. This was his response to my baldness. I realized that although doctors were used to seeing baldness from the chemo treatment, it affected them too. I still have the hairnet.

Well, it was a fun operation, as far as operations go, but the next day reality set in. A 16-inch tube was sticking out of my chest, requiring special care and attention. What had I accepted?

*R**emainder of* ***My Clinic Stay—Release*** ❧ I was now into my second week in the clinic, and my mother and I were stir crazy. Luckily, she could go out for the day; Lydia, Amy, or Cilla would keep me company. I was permitted to venture to a little square in the back of the hospital complex: five trees, six birds, and green grass. It was better than nothing, though. I figured maybe the Hickman was really an alarm that would go off if I wandered.

I had chemo number three, no more odd tests, and strange doctors. I read more now—during antibiotics and chemos too. I loved reading Tony Hillerman's mysteries; the wide open spaces of New Mexico and Arizona, and the calmness of Native American philosophy were soothing, a real escape. I also listened to music, especially my tape of *Enlightenment*. Best of all, I was excused from taking prednisone; Dr. Barnes felt that with the antibiotics, it was too much.

Lydia accompanied me to a class in Hickman care. A large crate of plastic foods was near us, used for teaching nutrition. Lydia picked up a plastic cup of fake orange juice. "Here, Darcy, how about a drink?" She turned it upside down. "Oops, I spilled it!" Next she picked up various fruits and began to bounce them on the floor. "Hey, Darcy, look at this! Bouncing bananas!" I highly recommend her attitude for these situations.

The weekend came. I missed seeing Ringo, but dogs are not allowed in the clinic, as a rule. Casey had considered disguising Ringo in a doctor's lab coat, but we figured his tail would give him away. Instead, my mother and I met Casey and Ringo out on a curb across the street from the hospital. We sat outside for about 20 minutes, pretending we were elsewhere.

In mid-June, I was released. I said goodbye to my nurses. "We should clone her," said Nurse Helen to Nurse Iris as she hugged me. "Take care of yourself,

RINGO SNEAKING IN AS A DOCTOR

Casey had considered disguising Ringo in a doctor's lab coat, but we figured his tail would give him away.

Darcy," said Nurse Iris, and she, too, hugged me good-bye.

Casey picked us up in his van. I preferred the security of driving with him, instead of taking a taxi (lucky big brother!). I was out, tagged like wildlife for tracking, but I was going home to paint.

Afterthoughts ∿ I discovered many valuable things in the clinic. It is a wonderful concept, a great alternative for those who don't require the hospital bed. Almost everyone there was receiving IV treatments. It was comforting to be sitting with others while we had our treatments. We had the option to share or not to share our experiences. We had some autonomy, which helped us keep our self-respect and personal space.

I never shared my situation with anyone, though—which I now somewhat regret. Most of the other patients either were older than me or had AIDS. The older ones paired off, and I felt a distance from the AIDS patients, for my illness had a cure and, sadly, theirs did not. It took all my strength and great effort to concentrate on my treatment. It was too much of an ordeal to try talking to others who were also ill. But I found it satisfying just to be together, alone in our individual battles against death.

I accepted that I had cancer and was determined to fight it with everything I had. I grew philosophical, often holding deep discussions with either Julia or Dr. Douglas. He had now become more than my physician, and we talked as if we had been close friends for years. The world seemed so fragile. How could humanity survive with all the strife and horror? I wanted to be honest and truthful, in my life and art. I wanted no part in game-playing or lies.

Throughout my confinement I managed to draw and paint in gouache (which is like thick watercolor), the first step in maintaining my sanity. The nurses kept me sane, too; I admired their gift of giving of themselves and listening to us patients. I once asked Nurse Iris how she handled the pressures of the job. "If I go home knowing that I've made at least one person smile or feel a little less pain, I am content," she replied. A modest statement, especially as I knew they did so much more.

Nurse Helen was a blessing. I felt relief every time I was assigned to her. She was a constant caring face amid all the chaos. She listened to my complaints and advised me about medical and personal problems, alert to my every mood. She had a wonderful sense of humor and we often joked together. I was lucky to receive her care.

I found out that doctors have their own protocol. They never criticize a colleague (unless, perhaps, if drunk—Dr. Loblolly certainly appeared so). They would disagree only with diagnoses or ideas on illness and treatment.

Last but not least, the clinic gave Dr. Barnes and me the chance to know each other better, with a little help from Dr. Douglas. During my stay in the clinic, Dr. Barnes mentioned the bone marrow transplant again, saying, "You'll get a two-headed Hickman, better for chemo during transplants."

"But I thought you said I was responding to this chemo real well. Why would I need a transplant too?" I asked anxiously.

"The Hickman is useful for transplants," he replied, avoiding my question. I felt a wall between us again.

Later when I saw Dr. Douglas, I asked, "Why doesn't Dr. Barnes tell me the truth about the transplant? I don't like not knowing his plans—either I get it or I don't."

"I will talk to him," answered Dr. Douglas.

The next day, as I sat quietly on the examination table, Dr. Barnes appeared and patted my knee, which amazed me. "How are you today?" he asked thoughtfully. "I guess it is hard to be cheerful all the time," he said, turning his back to get a seat.

I raised my eyebrows in question. This was the first time I had ever heard him acknowledge my efforts. I was surprised and responded cautiously, "Um, yeah, I'm okay."

"Oh, by the way, you won't need a transplant," he said casually. We caught each other's eyes and said nothing.

Dr. Barnes and I were now relating to each other on a more personal level, not just as doctor and patient. We were two stubborn people, but luckily for both of us we had similar senses of humor. This made him less reticent and me less defensive. He knew all the Marx Brothers jokes I threw at him. Their comedy of the absurd fit my situation best, for that was how my life seemed —absurd.

4

Life Around Chemotherapy

It was the middle of June and another hot summer in New York City. I was now halfway through my chemotherapy. I had lots of time to paint, but only after I figured out how to structure my life around chemo, 12 days on prednisone, and care of my Hickman. I ended up receiving my chemo treatments three weeks apart instead of two, because my WBC never climbed high enough in two weeks. Dr. Barnes had to balance the chemicals that killed the cancer without killing me in the process.

When I became more physically and mentally alert, I asked Dr. Barnes what my lymphoma and chemotherapy were called. The lymphoma was immunoblastic lymphoma, and the chemo was ProMACE CytaBOM. I had Dr. Barnes write them down for me; I felt I should know these words, although they meant little to me.

I chose to view my chemo as a cleanser of the cancer, rather than poison. Before each treatment, I'd relax in bed and psych myself up for the awful aftereffects of nausea and vomiting, which lasted from three to five hours. During the administering of chemo I fought any nausea that crept up—a mere whiff of rubbing alcohol could trigger it. Instead I tried to relax and make conversation with Nurse Kate, whose cheerful disposition and empathetic manner made the atmosphere tolerable.

Proper Care and Maintenance of "Mr. Hickman"

I asked Nurse Kate to help me with my Hickman by changing the caps every six weeks prior to a chemo treatment. I was too nervous to do it. More important, she checked my skin around the Hickman to see if I had infection or irritation. It put my mind at ease, for I worried quite a lot about caring for the Hickman.

Proper care and maintenance of my Hickman was an unavoidable ordeal. I had to flush the tubes three times a week with a solution of heparin to keep them from clogging. Injecting the heparin through the cap head was always a tense moment. I had to be sure there were no air bubbles in the syringe. As a precaution, Dr. Barnes told me to flush on Monday, Wednesday, and Friday. If anything went wrong, I would be able to get help (worry number one).

Showering was another ordeal. I removed the Band-Aids and let the Hickman hang down, making sure the clamps were closed so I would not bleed away. It reached as far as my crotch, and the heads would dangle and clack together. I cleansed the exit point with only water. Once finished, I gingerly stepped out, being careful not to snag it on anything. Dr. Leonard warned me that Hickmans can come out easily, from the slightest mishap (worry number two).

The next step was to clean and re-dress the exit point to keep it sterile and protected; infections were easily acquired too (worry number three).

Holding the Hickman with one hand, I wiped the skin around the exit point with rubbing alcohol followed by iodine, both applied with a sterile pad or swab. I covered the area with two 1-inch Band-Aids and wound and taped the rest of the tube over them, for the tape had irritated my skin. Also to lessen the irritation, I rotated the position of the Band-Aids each day, a trick I learned from Dr. Barnes. Wearing the Hickman in bow fashion was like wearing a badge pinned to my chest. Often the tape did not hold and the tube dangled. This happened usually during the night or while I was painting, interrupting the only times I could be somewhere else, lost in sleep or my art.

*T**he 12 Days of Prednisone* ∼ I took my temperature every day, sometimes three or four times when I suffered "fear of fever," which occurred during my 12 days of prednisone, especially when I was coming off it. Dr. Barnes warned me that I might have a low-grade fever on those days. Fever meant infection, which to me meant going back to the clinic.

Prednisone induced fear, hypertension, and extreme emotional sensitivity. I recall myself as bug-eyed on those days. I was charged up and slept little in spite of taking medication to help me sleep.

Coming off prednisone was a trip. And I do mean a trip—cold turkey time. I allowed two days for the process: one for my body and one for my mind. On the "body day" I requested no visitors and warned my mother I might be slightly paranoid and agitated. For about four hours or so my body lost control. I felt weak and giddy, and my insides shook like crazy. It began around midday. I lay still on my bed, flat on my back, and listened to music—usually Rachmaninoff's *Second Symphony*—until it passed.

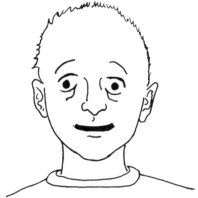

BUG-EYED DARCY ON
PREDNISONE

Prednisone induced fear, hypertension, and extreme emotional sensitivity. I recall myself as bug-eyed on those days.

On the "mind day" I was anxious, insecure, and possibly tearful, but physically okay. I handled it by seeing someone who made me feel secure. The first time it happened to be Dr. Leonard. I stopped off by his office after my weekly blood test to show him photos of my paintings and found myself talking a mile a minute. He smiled and graciously followed my conversation as if nothing were strange, even though I told him I was coming off the prednisone. We parted with a hug. I learned to reach out to whom and what made me feel secure, even on days on which I was not coming off prednisone. I no longer felt shy about asking for help.

Painting Through Treatment ~ My life was dictated by the treatment, and I planned my painting time around it. On release from the clinic I went to the Metropolitan Museum of Art with my mother and Casey to see a small exhibition of Eugene Delacroix's work. It was wonderful; his use of color, brushstroke, and subject matter gave me many ideas. Full of vitality and vibrance, his paintings reminded me of the life force in art.

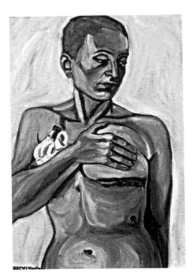

I began *The Lymphoma Series* immediately afterward and the paintings just flew out of me. *Pieta: Start of the Climb* was the first, and Amy said it reminded her of Giotto's work. So I pulled out my art books on Giotto, Velazquez (my favorite), Goya, and of course Delacroix. I began to search for the drama of life as depicted in art.

The paintings continued in rapid succession: *Seals I, In The Garden, Seals II, The Hospital Nightmare,* and *Self-Portrait with Hickman and Scar* [PLATE 7]. This last painting was a turning point for me, the first time I had ever painted myself nude. I photographed myself by

Self-Portrait With Hickman and Scar
[Plate 7, page 99]
Oil on canvas. July 1991. 16" x 24"

using a timer and worked from that image. Julia had suggested that I paint everything, and it was important to me not to be afraid to do so.

Next came *Doctor Triptych* **[PLATE 15],** a completely enjoyable experience. It gave me a sense of working on a large canvas, which my small apartment did not allow. I photographed my doctors, making sure they were not wearing their white lab coats. I was also careful to include their hands in the picture frame. I wanted them to be in bright colors against a dark background, contrasting the reassurance of reality against the fear of the unknown. In the pillars I placed symbolic images of each from my sketches done in the hospital: Dr. Barnes is the preacher, Dr. Douglas is sunshine, and Dr. Leonard is the knight with a sword.

This triptych is a tribute to the emotional and physical care my doctors gave me. I relied on them, not only as healers but also as strong men. I did not have a boyfriend or husband, although Casey and Alun were a wonderfully supportive brother and brother-in-law. My doctors knew how the lymphoma and its treatment functioned, so they understood exactly what I was going through. All three were caring and receptive enough to sense my need for a male protector at this most crucial time of my life. I asked them to see me not just as a patient but as Darcy the

Doctor Triptych (Dr. Barnes, Dr. Douglas, Dr. Leonard)
[Plate 15, page 107]
Oil on canvas. July 1991. Each panel 20" x 28"

artist, and as one who saw them as people too. I had complete faith in their abilities and judgments. They opened up to me and we became friends. This was a personal choice of theirs and mine. Not every doctor or patient wants that relationship. It just happened to be part of my method for survival.

The portrait *Nurse Helen* followed, also a tribute, to her and all the nurses who gave me so much of themselves. *Self-Portrait/Reflection*, based on my reflection in the lights of the OR, conveys all my vulnerability and dignity. I found that by admitting vulnerability I could accept and live with it.

Friends Triptych [PLATE 13] shows me between Fran and Julia, depicting the support they gave me through the look in their eyes. They are both in the arts too: Fran is a photographer and Julia is a poet. I've known both for some time and felt a strong connection with each—a recognition of self—on our first meeting. The painting is about that recognition and a way to tell them I love them, something one often doesn't say to a friend.

Rebirth [PLATE 12] is about accepting my body, exploring and learning to love myself. I found the concept of painting myself nude revealing in more ways than one. It was a way to show my new self, uninhibited by false modesty or

Friends Triptych (Fran, Darcy, Julia)
[Plate 13, page 105]
  Oil on canvas. August 1991. Each panel 14" x 20"

shame. I could not afford these feelings as I was baring my chest all the time. They also seemed such useless emotions. Since my head was bare, why not my body? After all, it was this body that did not give out on me that night in OR—I was proud of it.

*T*he Hickman Conspiracy ∾ Dr. Douglas was going away for his two-week summer vacation; I called for my weekly report. After reviewing everything he said, "Hang in there while I'm gone." Oddly, my hair started to grow back. Chemo number five was next, and I went in early for a CAT scan. My mother dared me to go hatless in the hospital, so I did. Some people stared, but nobody was unduly surprised and I managed to keep my head up. I asked Dr. Barnes about my growing hair, and he informed me that this, too, would fall out.

The next day I called Dr. Barnes for the results of the CAT scans, which were fine. I asked if the Hickman would be removed after all my chemos were done, as Dr. Douglas and I had concluded in the clinic.

"Not for six months to a year after all treatments, including radiation, are finished," he said calmly.

"What? Six months to a year! You must be kidding!"

"No, a year is the usual amount of time," he replied calmly.

"I can't wear this for a year! Do you know what it is like? How would you like to have to wear one?"

Needless to say, our conversation got nowhere. I hung up furious and upset. Why had he kept this from me? I felt he had not been honest by not informing me until I

Rebirth
[Plate 12, page 104]
Oil on canvas. August 1991. 18" x 24"

asked. My family listened in sympathy, but most felt one could not question the doctor's orders. I strongly disagreed.

Since Dr. Douglas was away, I called Dr. Leonard, then stopped by his office before the second half of chemo number five. We sat down and I asked him why I had to wear the Hickman for a year after treatment. Why had Dr. Barnes not informed me of this? "In case the lymphoma returns," he replied. Then, using a bit of reverse psychology, he said, "If you want, I can take it out now."

I felt belittled by this and replied, "No, I need it for my chemos." I tried again to express myself: "Why wear it just to see if the lymphoma returns?"

"We've no guarantee the lymphoma won't return. We can only do our best." He paused. "You know, nobody knows when their time will come. Why, I could get killed crossing the street tomorrow!"

"I realize what you are trying to say, but . . ." I felt abashed. He then told me of a former patient who had kept fighting a recurring cancer and how he was an example to everyone. I sighed in frustration and said, "I understand about fighting, but why wear the Hickman for so long? It is just a reminder—I don't think I could handle that." My eyes began to brim with tears.

"Do you want a therapist? I could ask Dr. Barnes for you." He reached for the phone.

"No! I mean no. I will ask him myself if I want one." I saw now that he had not understood what I was trying to say. Perhaps I wasn't so sure myself. Anyhow, I had to get out before I started to cry.

"I'm happy to listen to you, Darcy, but I don't think I can help you in this situation." He looked at me carefully.

"No, you've been very helpful. I must go get my chemo now." I raced out. I felt a complete failure. Was I not strong enough to handle the lymphoma returning? I needed therapy? What had happened to my inner strength—was that what was really bothering me?

My mother waited for me in the hallway, where I burst into tears. She tried her best to comfort me, and when I stopped crying we went to Dr. Barnes' office for my treatment.

Dr. Barnes called me into his office and, eyeing me warily, asked the routine questions. When he finished he said, "Is there anything else you want to tell me?"

"No." My sullen expression remained.

"Are you sure?" he asked cautiously.

"Yes." I kept my mouth shut and my tears back. I felt there was no point talking to him. We'd only argue, and that was something I couldn't do now.

I went in for chemo and on seeing my face Nurse Kate asked, "Are you all right? You seem kind of down today." I looked at her concerned expression and told her. "Dr. Barnes said I will have to wear the Hickman for a year and I don't want to. Dr. Leonard thought I might want to see a therapist to help me handle it. I'm lost. What do you think I should do?"

"You seem pretty strong—I don't think therapy would do much more for you. Don't you have a good relationship with Dr. Douglas? Can't you talk to him?"

"He is away now," I said quietly.

"Call him as soon as he returns and explain it to him."

I felt reassured by my conversation with Nurse Kate. Some control had returned to me. "Yes, you're right. Also he gives great hugs."

"Hugs are very important," she responded to my amazement. "People don't seem to realize that. You'll see—everything will work out fine." She patted my shoulder and smiled at me. I was impressed by her insight and grateful for her empathy.

*F*inally Dr. Douglas returned from his vacation, and I went to see him. I sat on the examination table and related the situation. "I felt confused and alone. Neither doctor seemed to understand. Dr. Leonard thought I was afraid of the lymphoma returning and suggested I see a therapist. But then I realized I wasn't afraid of the lymphoma returning—if it does, it does. I felt hurt and lied to about the Hickman. I couldn't talk to Dr. Barnes—we would only have yelled at each other—and you were away." We looked at each other. He thought carefully before he spoke. I looked down at the floor.

"First of all, I don't think you need therapy—you are very strong," he said. "Second, you must remember that it is your body, and you have the right to decide what happens to it."

"You know, I forget that it is my body." I was so often trying to do the right thing, to be a "good girl," that I was losing sight of something very important—me.

"I'm sure we can put the Hickman back in if the lymphoma returns," he continued. "I'll call Dr. Leonard and ask him. But I recommend you keep it in until the radiation is finished. It is easy to get infections then because your white blood count drops way down."

"Okay, that makes sense to me. Maybe the end of November?" I asked hopefully.

"That sounds good. Now just remember, it is your body."

"You always make me feel better," I said as I got off the examination table. "I don't feel so alone when you are around." We hugged as I held back my tears; his embrace seemed to erase all my sorrow and isolation.

I went to meet Julia for lunch. This was my first lunch in public, and I took off my hat in the restaurant. Hey, it's New York City—nobody noticed.

I often think back on the "Hickman conspiracy." It opened my eyes to doctors' methods. I realized Dr. Leonard could not say anything, and it was not his place to do so. As Dr. Barnes and I were so stubborn, we would only knock heads, and truth be known, I was still in awe of him. Dr. Douglas figured I would let them know how long I could handle it. He also gave me a valuable message. I had the right to say yes or no regarding my body.

The hurt I felt was a betrayal of trust. My doctors had not told me everything. If they had, would I have agreed to the Hickman? I will never know the answer to that question. The best I could do now was to decide for myself when to get the Hickman out and not be afraid to speak up for Darcy. I learned to evaluate the situation for myself. I had entered this treatment relying on my doctors' judgment for everything. Now I had to get involved, for there might be decisions that I would disagree with. I was fortunate that this was the only problem, and even more fortunate that I was given such good doctors. What if Doctor Loblolly had been in charge of my care? Perhaps I would have been too afraid ever to assess his judgment. I had a responsibility to take care of myself too.

My conversation with Dr. Leonard caused me to reflect on those less fortunate than me. The hostage crisis was unfolding, especially Terry Anderson's case, and I related strongly to it. What was a little Hickman bondage compared with seven years in captivity and no certainty of the next day's arriving?

I also found the perfect role model in Paul Tsongas. Although his lymphoma had been worse (it had spread), he survived and was running for president. More important, he was talking openly about his cancer; I admired that no end, as people are still so afraid of it. He is a brave and beautiful human being.

As for my Hickman, I found the best way to handle it was with humor. Dr. Douglas told me a Dr. Hickman from Seattle invented the device. I imagined a crazy man full of tubes, laughing away insanely. (All Hickman wearers draw your own picture of him now.)

At one point I had an idea to do a Hickman joke book. It never got anywhere, but there were a few good Hickman jokes. Lydia had two very visual ones that always made me laugh when I recalled them. The first was after I mentioned how I hated washing in the shower with the Hickman. She mimed me in the shower, lathering up my Hickman with lots of soap. "Got to get this Hickman really clean!" she said. The other was even better. Some of my family were visiting; it was somebody's birthday and wrapping paper and ribbon were lying about. Lydia took a ribbon and stuck it in her shirt. "Look, Ma, I got a Hickman, too!" A hush fell over the party, but I burst into laughter. It was a wonderful gesture of unity. None of them could know what it was like—they could only imagine the experience. Lydia, by the way, agreed with me about getting the Hickman out, encouraging and supporting my opinion.

After her ribbon joke, everyone else started to come up with one. Fran suggested that on entering someone's home I'd ask, "Excuse me, where can I plug in?" I wanted to write an "Ode to the Hickman" à la Percy Dovetonsils (Ernie Kovacs' dandy poet caricature). I got as far as this:

ODE TO THE HICKMAN
by Darcy Dovetonsils

Oh my little Hickman, when I flush your tubes
All the clicking and clacking as you dangle between my boobs.
I detest you most when I am in the shower.
I wish you would get out—our relationship has gone sour!

~

Pretty bad, I admit, but Hickman wearers will appreciate it. My favorite joke was to hit my Hickman and say, "One to beam up!" Yes, *Star Trek* was handy for many jokes besides my "bald buddy."

I was finally able to wear a bra again, because it no longer irritated my scar. Dr. Barnes, on seeing me bare-chested after I first had the Hickman put in, said, "Some people tuck the Hickman in their bras."(I still laugh over that one—I believe he meant to say "women.") I dubbed them Hickman Holders. If I was painting and the tape came undone, the Hickman Holder held it in place and I was not interrupted. Sorry, guys, I have no suggestions for you.

A Little Help From Family and Friends ～ A large family is wonderful in times of crisis. All pitch in whenever and however they can. Each member of my family gave me so much love and support that I could face the cancer with courage. My father often drove into Brooklyn with his wife and sons to meet me at a local diner. He'd had triple-bypass surgery, and we often compared notes about our illnesses. He had bought me the Walkman for the hospital stay, as he knew what a comfort music was.

My siblings were incredibly supportive: all gave of themselves tremendously, keeping their fears and worries from me. If they did not visit, they called. My youngest sister, Emily, called me every day and always made me laugh. She is quick with words and a sympathetic listener. Lydia, next in age, was my personal shopper; she bought me clothes and hats to keep up my feminine morale. I've mentioned her humor, but she also has a special natural warmth. Lydia's husband, Alun, listened and asked me many questions about my discoveries. We had philosophical talks about life, too. He is like another brother to me.

Cilla, my buddy in our family buddy system, was an excellent listener to my medical complaints and great to share silly stories with; she was always ready to help in any way. Amy, my big sister, would come at the drop of a hat if I needed her to buy groceries, pick up prescriptions, or just keep me company. She is gracious and giving, wanting only to be helpful. My brother Casey (only a year older than me) was patient and understanding and invariably a funny guy. As we are both artists, we have much in common. He often knew what to say or do; an example is his gift of the tape *Enlightenment*.

My mother was the best listener and most patient person. She was always there with me and comforted me every time I cried (which I often did when only she was around). She had experienced life and death issues and already knew what I was just learning. She boosted my morale and kept my outlook on the future optimistic.

Looking at how my family supported me, I find that I mention two characteristics over and over: being a good listener and having a sense of humor. Cultivating these two qualities, plus the essential ingredient of love, is the most important way in which one can help a person with a critical illness. I have been blessed with a family who gives me all these things.

I was also given the love and support of other relatives and of many other friends besides Julia, Fran, Donna, and Kevin—people who wrote or phoned if it was not possible to see me. I was lucky to have kept in touch with all but a few of my friends.

Often a person facing a serious illness loses friends. Some people are either too scared or unable to handle the situation. I was fortunate not to know many like this.

One special friend never saw a bald lady with a tube hanging out of her chest; he just saw Darcy. That was Ringo. My greatest pleasure was to have him kiss me with his big slobbering tongue and sit on my feet. Animals do not discriminate: they give love freely. I highly recommend having a pet around to cure depression.

The best gift I received was a poem by Julia, titled simply *Lymphoma Poem*. After I read it I cried in front of her for the first time. It was so full of beauty and love I could not do otherwise.

I finished chemotherapy at the end of August. I now had some time to recuperate from chemo and to paint. The first part of my treatment was done and radiation was next—meanwhile time off for good behavior.

RINGO SITTING ON MY FEET

One special friend never saw a bald lady with a tube hanging out of her chest; he just saw Darcy. That was Ringo.

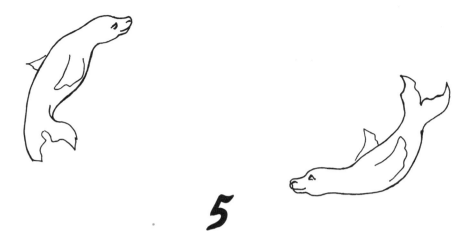

5

In the Fall We Harvest and Radiate, or It Ain't Over Yet

The Lymphoma Series Continues ⌒ September began quietly. I made only a couple of visits to the hospital for tests: a CAT scan of my chest and abdomen and a gallium scan (an injection of a tracer into my veins) to ensure that there were no other signs of the lymphoma in my body. They turned up negative and I continued to paint.

My *Dramatic Body* *[PLATE 9]* depicts my body undergoing chemo. Often I try to find words to describe the experience, and the best I can think of are inner turmoil or chaos. The chemo was a foreign matter that my body did not want, yet my mind very much did want. How else could I fight the cancer?

I created two more paintings at the suggestion of others, both from pencil sketches. I painted *The Illusion in the X-Ray Room* at Casey's suggestion and *The Three Musketeers* at Fran's suggestion. *The Three Musketeers* was a big success, especially with the doctors. I wanted to get just the right expressions for each: Dr. Leonard is complacent, Dr. Douglas is laughing away, and Dr. Barnes is grinning over his shoulder—the chemodoc who slew the lymphoma dragon. Everyone laughed when they saw it (remember, laughter is the best medicine).

I ran out of ideas for *The Lymphoma Series*, so I returned to painting nature. The *Brooklyn Botanical Gardens* was a great source for material—a real lifesaver, too. My mother and I managed to go to the gardens at least once a week throughout my chemos. I found nature therapeutic, its continuity reassuring and life-affirming. The first landscape I did after my illness reflected my amazement and joy at seeing nature's beauty *[PLATE 19]*.

Preparing for the Harvest ～ In mid-September I had a checkup with Dr. Barnes. "You are no fun anymore," he said as we sat in his office.

"Would you rather I leave?"

"Seriously, you are doing very well. The next step is radiation. Your tests are all negative, but I'd rather you had it as a precautionary measure."

"Yes, Dr. Douglas said the same thing, and I agree." I wanted to assert myself here, as I now was aware that I had a right to. He explained that I would receive it in the hospital from a Dr. Blake as soon as my WBC rose and after I had a bone

My Dramatic Body
[Plate 9, page 101]
Oil on canvas. August 1991. 18" x 28"

marrow harvest. The harvest was a procedure of removing the white blood cells from the bone marrow in the pelvic bones for storage, in case the lymphoma returned and I needed a transplant. I had read of Paul Tsongas having undergone one—a massive dose of chemo, which kills everything, followed by a reinjection of white blood cells to help recuperate from the chemo. We had reviewed this earlier, so I was prepared. "Okay. Will you do it?" I asked hopefully.

"No. We've no facilities to store bone marrow here. You'll have to go to another hospital."

"Another hospital? Couldn't you store them under your desk?" That old trouble-maker, fear, had returned. The idea of being in a different hospital and away from my doctors terrified me. But I was too embarrassed to voice my fears to Dr. Barnes.

We entered an examination room, where he performed a bone marrow biopsy on me—I felt little pain because I had no fear about this procedure. I would take the results to the other hospital. Dr. Barnes explained what the harvest would entail and how I would feel. They would anesthetize me, as the procedure was painful, and I would be sore for about a week, as if "someone had pulled a chair out from under you" (his words). Radiation treatment could begin after that.

Now I was really scared. Not only would I be away from my doctors and in another hospital, I would be knocked out too. Irrational fear from my earlier experience in the hospital made it seem horrible. How would my body perform under the anesthetic? At that moment I could not find words to voice this fear.

Brooklyn Botanical Gardens
[Plate 19, page 111]
Oil on canvas. September 1991. 30" x 20"

Meeting Dr. Crackers One and Two ∿ An appointment was made at the other hospital and Casey drove me there. We had some difficulty finding it, and then we had to battle our way through a maze of identical hallways and floors until we found the oncologist's office. We waited an hour.

Two doctors walked in, both sporting beards and speaking in foreign accents. One had a box of crackers sticking out of his lab coat pocket.

"That must be Dr. Crackers," whispered Casey.

"And Dr. Crackers Number Two," I replied.

A nurse came out. "Ms. Lynn, your doctors are ready to see you now." I followed her into an examination room, where the two Dr. Crackers were waiting for me. Dr. Crackers One, distinguished by a dark beard and hair, had me sit on the table and began to examine me fully clothed.

"I listen to your heart and lungs," he said, and stuck his stethoscope under my bra. After a minute he pulled it away, letting my bra snap on my scar. I grimaced at him. "Oh, sorry." He sat down and took out a pen and clipboard. "Now I ask about your history," he stated.

"My history?" I asked, confused.

"He means your illness," chirped Dr. Crackers Two, who had a snow-white beard and hair.

"Yes. How old are you and when you last have chemo?" said Dr. Crackers One as he continued his inquiry.

"I am thirty-five and I last had chemo at the end of August."

"You look only twenty-five! You start radiation yet?"

"Thanks. No I haven't. Dr. Barnes wanted me to wait until after the harvest."

"Why you wait? We can give you radiation here while you have harvest!"

"Well . . . I'll have to ask Dr. Barnes about that."

"You still have Hickman—why?"

"Dr. Barnes wants me to keep it in as a precautionary measure." I started to feel threatened.

"You get more chemo? You get transplant?" he asked eagerly.

"No!" I snapped. "No, I am just getting a harvest." Now I felt threatened and nervous: it was beginning to feel like an interrogation.

"Hmmm . . . you have operation before?"

"Yes, the biopsy."

"I look at incision." He rose and came to me with Dr. Crackers Two following.

"See? Dr. Leonard performed it here." I lifted my shirt and bra.

"Hmmm . . . good job. What happened?"

"It was a biopsy . . ." Words failed me. How could I begin to explain what had happened to me that night in OR? "Call and ask him."

"Ah, we see. Most interesting," said Dr. Crackers Two, trying to smooth things over. His English was slightly better than that of Dr. Crackers One. It would have been funny, except that it was my body they were talking about. Luckily their assistant, Nurse Selena, a beautiful woman from Jamaica, later reviewed everything with me.

"We need to schedule you for another bone marrow biopsy before harvest," pronounced Dr. Crackers One and took out his appointment book.

"But Dr. Barnes just did one—you've the results right in front of you," I said nervously.

"Always we do biopsy here. It is necessary . . . he will do it." Dr. Crackers One pointed to his pal.

"Oh great, " I said under my breath. "When will I have the harvest?"

"Only we do harvests on Fridays. Let me see." He looked at his book. "You get harvest on October 11th, so biopsy will be . . . October 7th, Monday."

"Is that the earliest—three weeks?"

"Yes, you check in on the 10th and we perform harvest early next morning, 8:00 perhaps. If you well enough after, you go home same day!" he concluded, smiling. I hurried out to Casey once I had finished. "Let's get out of here. I can barely understand them." I was upset, angry, and scared. We left quickly.

Well, not that quickly. Once more we had to contend with the maze of identical

_RESOLVED

hallways and floors, and were going in circles at one point. Casey turned to me and said, "I'll just open a window in one of these rooms and we can climb out." We managed to escape, and Casey made jokes on the drive back to keep me laughing all the way home.

Meeting Dr. Blake ∼ I had an appointment with Dr. Blake, who would manage my radiation after the harvest. A small, alert, and spunky woman, close to my age, came out and shook hands. "Hello, I am Dr. Blake and I will be your radiologist" *[PLATE 16]*. I liked the looks of her and immediately felt we would get on. I think she felt the same. "I'd like to give you a complete examination and then explain the treatment." She led me to an examination room, where I undressed completely except for my panties. Then both she and an intern took turns examining me. Right away I noticed that her touch was much gentler than his. Once they finished, they asked questions about my biopsy.

"Can I see the scar again?" asked the intern. "What a great job!" He admired it.

"Thanks, I'll tell Dr. Leonard you said so." By now I was tired of being cross-examined and prodded. They both inquired about what had actually happened

Dr. Blake
[Plate 16, page 108]
Oil on canvas. Dec 1991. 20" x 28"

~ 68

during the biopsy, and again feeling defensive (though I didn't know why), I said, "You can call Dr. Leonard and ask him. He's right here in the hospital."

Dr. Blake sensed my discomfort. "I know Dr. Leonard—I can call him. Now, I sent your CAT scans to a specialist for a second opinion. He felt you should get the full regimen, twenty-four treatments in all." The end of all this seemed further and further away. She continued, "You will have it every day, except weekends, and I'd like you to get a blood test twice a week, a finger stick only, to monitor your WBC. After your harvest we will paint the tattoos on you to map out where you will receive radiation. You will have eight treatments over all of the left side of your chest and most of your right." She showed me where on herself. "I will mask out the area around your Hickman so you won't risk an infection there. The final sixteen treatments will be in a much smaller area—around your sternum, where the tumor was. This should guarantee that we destroy any lingering cancer cells."

I got dressed and she informed me of the risks of radiation: the possibility of lung and heart damage and the chance of breast cancer. I was amazed that she kept nothing from me. She then explained that the risks were small but that I should be aware of them. The side effects would be fatigue and perhaps nausea. She concluded, "If you have any questions or wish to talk to me about all this, please feel free to call me anytime."

Dr. Blake was my only woman doctor, and I found her approach to be different from that of my male doctors. She not only gave me the complete picture, both the good and the bad, she let me know that she was always available. By telling me everything she was respecting my views—it was my body—and by being accessible she closed the distance usually created between doctor and patient.

My male doctors never gave me the whole picture, but as my protectors they must have wanted to shelter me from what they deemed too difficult for me to handle. I don't remember any of them actually inviting me to call them at any time, although if I had I know they would have listened to me. I often felt I would interrupt the busy doctors, forgetting my right to ask them anything about my health. Dr. Douglas, though, was an exception; I had phoned many times with questions, and he told me I must call him once a week to report in.

***D**ealing With Fear* ∼ I had two more tests to see if chemo had damaged my lungs or heart, and both turned out negative. I went in for the bone marrow biopsy on October 7th; Dr. Crackers Two had me lie on my stomach, which caused much more pain than if I had been on my side. Once again I felt anxious and scared about the harvest.

I called Dr. Barnes to inform him of the harvest date and confirm when radiation should start. I also told him he did the best bone marrow biopsies. He thanked me with genuine pride and modesty. I wanted to tell him I was scared about the harvest but felt he was too busy to hear such talk.

I decided to tell Dr. Douglas instead. I was so nervous I decided to see Julia too. Since my stay in the clinic, I found that both Dr. Douglas and Julia gave me courage. I felt a special bond with them, as if they could see into my soul and bring out my strength.

This was the first time I had ever gone to see Dr. Douglas just to talk to him, and I felt shy in doing so. I wavered in the waiting room and I almost left, but he appeared at that moment and showed me into his office. We sat down facing each other—no desk between us—and I told him my fears. He explained that from what he'd heard, it was a very good hospital. I still felt anxious and said, "I know it's irrational, but I'm scared of being knocked out during the procedure. I always thought I was brave, but now I feel like such a coward."

"You are brave, but you need anesthetic because it is such a painful procedure."

"I know that. I just needed to voice it, and to see you."

"I wish I could help you more." He looked at me sweetly.

"You have. Seeing you helps me very much. May I call you afterward?"

"Yes, please do. I want to know how it goes."

"Can I have a hug now?" We both rose.

"No, but can *I* have a hug now?" he said as he held his arms open.

I met Julia for lunch. In the restaurant she pulled out a tiny pin of a bee and said, "I know this is silly, but maybe it will give you strength."

"It is wonderful, Julia!" I exclaimed. "I'll stick the Dr. Crackers with it if they give me trouble."

***T**he Harvest* ∾ Thursday came and Casey and my mother took me to the other hospital. After they left I set myself up in my hospital bed with Van Morrison playing on the Walkman and a Tony Hillerman mystery to read. My Hickman was hooked up to an IV on a rack, and nurses, nurse's aides, and doctors came in and out to poke and prod me. Just like old times. I shared the room with a woman who spoke only Spanish; we managed a hello, but that was all.

Amy called and we spoke of tomorrow's plans. She and my mother would be waiting for me after the operation. I attempted to sleep and was awakened by the resident doctor, who gave me a complete—and I do mean complete—physical examination.

At 7:00 AM the stretcher arrived. Once again I climbed on, wearing only a hospital gown. As I was rolled through the maze of hallways I thought of the time before, only now I felt utterly alone. The orderly rolled me into a spot, as if parking a car, in the OR while a room was readied. A nurse wheeled me into a glass-partitioned operating room. Suddenly I was surrounded by nurses and doctors. The anesthetist and his assistant approached me as Dr. Crackers Two hovered in the background, eagerly observing everything.

"We will insert the needle in her left hand, I think," said the anesthetist to his assistant. She began to poke and stab about for a suitable vein.

"How come you don't use Hickman?" asked Dr. Crackers Two.

"Because you doctors don't like us to," replied the assistant. (I noticed, as time went on, that no one ever used the Hickman for drawing blood either—in fact, it was never used again.)

I turned my eyes to the operating table; a huge pillow-type contraption lay on top of it. I would soon be on my stomach on top of that. How embarrassing—good thing I would be knocked out. At the end of the table, a nurse was rolling up little circular tubes. I thought they were to put around my ankles.

Dr. Crackers One came in wearing his blue doctor's uniform, a hair net, and goggles, and he was grinning from ear to ear. "How old are you?" he asked again.

"Thirty-five." I felt groggy: the anesthetic was beginning to take effect.

"You look twenty," he said and came closer.

"Sure, getting younger every day," I thought to myself.

"Nothing to worry about—it will be a piece of cake!" he said.

The assistant whispered in my ear, "Easy for him to say." We grinned at each other. I started to fade and prayed I would not have trouble breathing. Then I blacked out.

I awoke in the recovery room, stiff and sore in my lower back. I was wrapped up in a blanket like a papoose. A nurse put an oxygen mask on me. The plastic smelled and I saw no seals, but I was immensely proud of myself. I had conquered the fear and was pleased with my body for not giving out on me. The assistant anesthetist appeared on my other side. "Are you okay, hon?" she asked.

"Yes, and I'm so glad it's over," I gasped.

"Wow, you woke up smiling! I wish more people did."

"I'm very happy." Tears welled up in my eyes as I smiled at her.

"Do you know who you are and where you are?" she asked.

"Oh yes."

"That is what I like, a patient who is happy and alert!" She left and the nurse took over.

"Let's see if you've anything on." She unraveled my papoose. "No. Here, I'll put this gown on you." I began to weep, unable to contain my tears any longer. She took my hand and held it. "Anxious?" she asked calmly.

"Yes, I was nervous about it." I stopped crying.

"My brother had one here last week. He has leukemia." She sounded distant.

"Oh? Is he okay?" Leukemia sounded far worse than lymphoma. But it was a comfort to imagine a young man going through the same procedure. I did not feel so alone.

"Yes, in fact he is getting married in a few months," she replied in the same weary tone, but her face looked full of pain.

"How wonderful! Congratulate him for me."

My blood pressure had dropped somewhat and I felt nauseated. They rang Nurse Selena to bring some of my red blood, which had been saved from the operation, to reinject to raise my blood pressure. She arrived with a clear plastic, tire-shaped tube full of my red blood. I averted my eyes. I was bothered by the idea of my own blood hanging beside me. I told myself it was returning to me, not going away. The oxygen mask was removed and my blood pressure slowly began to climb. They were preparing to return me to my room when a knifing victim was wheeled right next to me.

He was a huge man, unconscious, thrashing about and occasionally shouting out loud, completely unaware of his situation. He was naked except for the hospital gown, which half covered him, and I saw the knife wound in his chest. He had a tube up his nose and one down his throat; the nurses, interns, and a doctor tried to restrain him. I stared in fascination and horror. I thought how I must have looked the same when my family saw me full of tubes. I felt compassion for this man, ignorant of the things happening to him yet compelled to fight and shout. A nurse yelled his name into his ear, trying to rouse him from the nightmare. Several male interns, nurses, and doctors attempted to stick an IV needle in his ankle as they tied him down.

Then they remembered me and wheeled me back to my room, where my mother and Amy waited. The other patient had left and they had been waiting a couple of hours at least. A nurse helped me with a commode; my bladder was at the bursting point. I then asked her to remove the IV from my left hand, which had swollen up completely. She left to get permission to do so. Meanwhile I called Dr. Douglas and told him how I was. After that the nurse removed the IV from my hand and I sat in bed chatting away with my mother and Amy while I ate some food; we were all happy and relieved. The Dr. Crackers came in around 4:00 PM.

"How you feeling?" asked Dr. Crackers One as he examined my dressing and listened to my heart and lungs.

"Great, I'm glad it's over."

"You look fine. I think you can go home today."

"Really? When?"

"Six o'clock is good," he replied, looking at his watch. He turned to his pal and the mood suddenly changed. The Dr. Crackers started to tell jokes, American style. They sounded like the "Two Wild and Crazy Guys" from the television show *Saturday Night Live*. My mother and Amy stared open-mouthed, trying desperately not to laugh. Dr. Crackers Two said something like, "Got a dollar?" It sounded like one of our family jokes and I wondered if I had made any jokes during the operation. Before they left, he contributed one more joke: "We got enough white blood cells for four transplants!"

"Gosh, thanks," I replied sarcastically.

"Hey, she don't want to hear that!" said Dr. Crackers One. They left, pleased with themselves for their mastery of American humor. End of harvest. I was sore for two weeks afterward. I was full of holes and counted them all *[PLATE 10]* (like the words in the Beatles song, "A Day in the Life").

THE DR. CRACKERS, TWO
WILD & CRAZY GUYS

The Dr. Crackers started to tell jokes, American style. They sounded like the "Two Wild and Crazy Guys" from the television show Saturday Night Live.

Radiation Therapy, or "Zaptime" ⌢ Radiation could now begin. I hobbled into the hospital so they could paint fuchsia T and L marks on my chest *[PLATE 11]*. I met the technicians, Julio and Marie, both lovely, warm people. Julio scheduled me for 12:00 noon every day, starting on Thursday, October 17th. It would be some time before I finished. I bought some turtleneck shirts to hide the T on my neck; it was my vampire bite.

Radiation treatment consisted of lots of waiting: one hour on bad days, 20 minutes on good days. I read a lot. The actual treatment lasted only about one minute. I stripped to the waist and donned a hospital gown. Julio and Marie set me up on a metal table with a bedsheet over it, uncovered my chest, and aligned the machine with my tattoos. A graph of plastic sheeting was placed under the lens of the machine with lead blocks to protect certain areas from the radiation. A strap was put around my waist, to hold me in place rather than to restrain me. I received radiation for 30 seconds on my chest. The machine was then turned under me and I received another 30 seconds on my back through the table.

The patient receiving treatment lies perfectly still and alone in the dark; communication with the technicians is through an intercom system. I found being

After the Harvest
[Plate 10, page 102]
Oil on canvas. November 1991.
16" x 22"

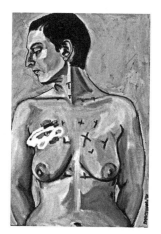

Self-Portrait With Radiation Tattoos
[Plate 11, page 103]
Oil on canvas. November 1991.
14" x 22"

alone with a machine much more difficult than chemo, because there was no one to talk to and the machine is so impersonal. Thank goodness radiation is quick. Even so, toward the end I had to fight the urge to jump off the table, scream, and run away. Fortunately Julio and Marie liked to joke around with me, and that helped me survive the treatment.

At home, my only concern was to be sure to shower with my back to the spout. I had to keep my chest as dry as possible. I went alone for my treatments, taking a subway and bus both ways. I enjoyed the freedom and my ability to handle it. After I had six treatments they painted me with more T and L marks, this time deep blue. It was for the area around my sternum; thus I was covered with two sets of tattoos for about one week.

Radiation treatment was uneventful. Dr. Blake checked me once a week, and I got finger-stick blood tests twice a week. The blood tests soon became a daily event, because my WBC dropped so low—and sometimes the machine broke down, which set me back a day.

I remember one incident well. Just after I received my second set of tattoos, I started to run a low-grade fever. Dr. Blake had me notify Dr. Barnes, who asked me to come in early the next day for urine and blood cultures, and a chest x-ray—I could be having another infection.

I was to report to him after my noon zap (my word for radiation) for a check-up. Of course there was a delay that day, and everyone's zap was an hour later. I called Dr. Barnes' secretary to inform her, and she suggested that I eat something first. After a light lunch (I was quite anxious), I went to Dr. Barnes' office. I entered the examination room and put on a gown. When he came in I warned, "I am rather colorful now."

"I can see you are!" he said, opening my gown. "Well, you should be able to appreciate that."

"I do, I do."

"Your x-rays show nothing. I think we will wait to see if your cultures show anything before I decide to put you on antibiotics," he said as he listened to my lungs.

"IV antibiotics?" I asked warily, afraid I would be sent back to the clinic.

"No, it would be oral antibiotics—if you need them."

"Good." Feeling relieved, I asked innocently, "You mean we can't go to Washington Square Park?"

"Sure we can go to Washington Square Park," he said as he listened to me and my heart at the same time. "Why are we going there?" He gave me a quizzical look.

"To get drugs." I saw us sitting in the park, me with my Hickman hooked up to an IV and him in his lab coat, trying to obtain "drugs."

"Oh, right. I got you. No, we don't need to go there." By now Dr. Barnes was used to Darcy jokes. "I need to take your temperature now."

"Uh-oh. I just drank something 20 minutes ago."

"You want me to take it the other way?" Exasperation crossed his face as I sheepishly looked at him. "Wait, I'll use my mother's method." He wiped his palms dry on his lab coat. First he placed his hands on my temples and then on my forehead; we tried not to laugh. "Well, you aren't burning up!" He sat down to write something. "Call me Monday—I'll have the lab test results by then."

Dr. Barnes and I looking for "drugs" in Washington Square Park.

"Anything else I should know?" I asked, grinning at him.

"You drive me crazy." He looked up to see how I responded.

"Hey, that's my job."

I called him Monday for the test results. He told me they were all negative and that I must have had a mild infection. I said, "You know what? After I saw you my fever went away. I think you have the power of 'laying on hands.' "

"Yes, well that's one of my many talents."

"I'm going to tell all the newspapers, and you'll have swarms of people coming to see you."

"Great, just the sort of patients I don't want."

My final treatment was November 22nd; my total zap ordeal, including delays, lasted six weeks. After my last zap I went on a hugging spree: I hugged Julio, Marie, and Dr. Blake after she examined me. Dr. Douglas had to wait until the next week.

At home, the first thing I did was to carefully wash off my tattoos—my skin was extremely sensitive. The tattoos plus the Hickman and scar made me feel inhuman, like a branded sheep. My hair had also grown back enough to be fashionable. Not that I minded being bald—it was just some of the stares I received, a few with disgust, that bothered me.

Thanksgiving was the best I ever had, something to be really thankful for. Now that all my treatments were done, I thought I had only the Hickman to deal with. I was wrong.

6

The Slow Journey to Recovery

It was December and I wanted to catch up on my art; during zaptime I had only managed to paint *After the Harvest* and *Self-Portrait With Radiation Tattoos* because I was so tired all the time. Next I did the portrait of Dr. Blake, and when I gave her a photo of it she exclaimed, "I've got seals too!" She was also impressed with my other work and thanked me for including her in the series.

I was still married to Mr. Hickman and decided it was time for a divorce. But I was anxious about telling Dr. Barnes, and asked Dr. Douglas how I might approach the subject. He replied, "Just tell him you want it out."

At my checkup with Dr. Barnes I pointed to the Hickman and said, "I want this out."

"Can't you keep it in a bit longer?" he pleaded with me. I was determined and refused. "Well, it's your body, but I think you should keep it in," he said, giving me his doctor look (every doctor has one—the removed, professional look).

I grew defensive and told him I'd spoken with Dr. Douglas and knew I could have it out now. He mumbled something as we walked to an examination room, then tossed me a paper gown and grumbled, "I'll be right back." When he returned

I was waiting on the examination table. He said, "I can't always get what I want."

"Thank you." Relief flooded through me. I hated any confrontation with him.

"Don't think I go home at night saying, 'Ha, ha! Darcy has to keep the Hickman in!'" he blurted out, to my surprise.

I wrapped my arms around his waist and said, "I would never think that!" He must have been taken aback, but I had been meaning to do that for a long time.

Dr. Barnes was now on my list of hugging victims. My picture was now probably in every post office with the caption: Wanted for Hugging Doctors, Nurses. . . You Name It!

I got home, kicked my heels in the air, and shouted, "Terry Anderson and I are free!" He had been released two weeks earlier after seven years as a hostage. I hung a picture of him smiling on my wall; it became a great comfort in the following months.

WANTED: FOR HUGGING DOCTORS, NURSES,... YOU NAME IT!

Dr. Barnes was now on my list of hugging victims. My picture was now probably in every post office.

Christmas was coming, and I decided to wait until mid-January to have my Hickman removed. I wanted to make sure my WBC had climbed enough and that no infections would occur. That meant flushing my tubes on Christmas Day, and so I sang, "I flushed my tubes on Christmas Day . . ."—one last Hickman joke.

*D*r. *Leonard Declares Me Free* ∽ Hickman removal day was January 14, 1992, a day to remember. I sat in Dr. Leonard's waiting room for a long time, until he arrived and said, "Dr. Barnes doesn't want you to have it out yet." He spoke sternly and gave me his doctor look.

"I know, but I want it out today." I heard my voice quiver and could feel my face flush.

"As soon as the room is free, then," he said curtly and left.

I sighed in relief. These men sure made things difficult. A nurse ushered me into the examination room, told me to change, and left. I stripped to the waist, put on a paper gown, and sat on the table to wait. I wondered if he was trying to make me change my mind, and I grew anxious. At last he came in, wearing his grin. "Sorry, a long phone call. How are you?"

"Fine, eager to get this out." His sudden switch in manner surprised and confused me.

"Yeah, I can imagine. Okay, lie back." He took out a syringe and said, "I'll just numb the area first." He stuck the needle in my chest and waited for the anesthetic to work. I asked how he was and he replied, "Tired—everyone is so sick this winter. How's your art going?"

"Good. I'm trying to find a gallery to exhibit *The Lymphoma Series*, but everyone says it's too personal!"

"Don't give up, and let me know when you get a show—I'll come." He began to gently tug the Hickman. "Let me know if I hurt you."

"No, I feel nothing." He continued to tug. "At this rate you may have to put your knee on my chest and pull."

"Perhaps." He smiled. "Your body is just used to the Hickman."

"Wonderful—just what I need."

"Wait, it's coming out . . . here, it's out." He applied pressure to the vein where it had been. I had images of blood spurting everywhere. "Want to see it?" he asked.

"Yes." There wasn't much to see, just more tube with a notch to keep it in place under the skin. "I should keep it and attach it to my *Self-Portrait / Reflection*."

"That's too gross." He grimaced at me while still applying pressure to my vein.

"You think it's gross? But you're a doctor!"

"As me, I think it's gross. Put your hand here while I throw this thing out."

Dr. Leonard was full of surprises: his change of manner after he had done his "doctor duty" and now his reaction to my suggestion about the Hickman. Doctors don't often show their personal side, but then most doctors don't have me for a patient. I sat up and dressed as he continued to apply pressure, moving slowly as if in a dream.

"A bit anticlimactic, huh?" he asked, helping me to dress.

"Yeah." I now felt it was time to ask him once more what had happened that night in OR, as everyone kept asking me. But I was too afraid to ask about the incision under my breast—why it was there and why it was so big. He repeated what he had said in the hospital: he had performed the biopsy, and they had put me on the respirator as they were afraid the tumor had put too much pressure on my heart and lungs. He finished by saying, "When Dr. Barnes gave you the chemo he had to guess what type to use. He guessed right too, because your tumor shrank 70%."

"I remember." I mused about that event. "He's my hero."

"Yeah, he's a great guy."

He turned to clean up, and I jumped off the table with my arms wide open and cleared my throat. He turned around and I hugged him. He reciprocated with a big bear hug. "Thank you for everything, and I do mean everything!"

"You are quite welcome," he replied modestly.

So off I went; Dr. Leonard had declared me a free woman. I was sure everything would be fine now, but I could not have been more wrong.

Depression and Those Damned Hormones

I fell into a deep depression. I tried rationalizing it, telling myself I was missing all the attention from my doctors and the people around me, but I could not rid myself of a growing darkness in my soul. I decided I had better talk to Dr. Douglas.

"I don't understand why I am so depressed," I said.

"It is natural for people to go through a depression after recovering from a serious illness."

"But why? I should be happy—it's all over and I'm free."

"After spending so much time fighting your illness and handling the treatment, it all ends and you feel abandoned."

"Yes, I figured that part. But why this inner darkness?" I braced myself to ask the next question. "Did I almost die?"

"Let's just say you came real close to biting the dust."

"I keep thinking about it." I felt relieved to admit it aloud. "The fact that I had almost died is finally registering."

"You were lucky and survived. Look at it this way: you were in the sick world and now you are in the well world."

"That's a good way to put it. You know what else? I'm going to miss all you guys. I actually liked talking to you about my art, too." I felt shy saying this.

"Well, you'll just have to make social visits."

"I guess." I wondered how I could just visit doctors. They are always so busy. But I returned to my depression. "Why do I feel such an inner darkness?"

He grew concerned. "You've got to get busy doing something."

I told him how I had been busy gallery hunting and joining art groups. But I felt I was losing everything—my new self, my new knowledge, my new friends—

and I did not know how to express it. He stood deep in thought, then suddenly he said, "You know, I can get real angry. You haven't seen me, but I can!" He stared at me with his doctor look. I was surprised, a bit hurt, and scared. I replied, "You get angry at me? I would just cry if you yelled at me." I smiled lamely.

He realized anger would not snap me out of it, or perhaps we had just misunderstood each other. "What is it you've always wanted to do?" he asked in a softer voice.

"To tell the truth, I'd like to get married and have a baby. I am already an artist."

"Then that is what you should do."

"Know anyone?"

"Hmmm, I'll have to think."

"Boy, I sure do ask a lot of you, don't I?"

"Yeah, besides doctor and therapist, I'll be a matchmaker!"

Once more I mentioned seeing a therapist for my inner depression. He still felt I was strong enough to handle it and suggested I paint it out, which is exactly what I did.

I painted, pastelled, and drew. I drew black charcoal pictures of myself in a world of darkness, using Goya's black paintings as an inspiration. I had to reflect on that night in OR, my determination to live and to see who I had become.

Recovery also involved getting my hormones back in balance. My menstrual cycle had stopped; chemo often stops it, sometimes permanently. My first period after chemo was eight months after my last—exactly the time I had the Hickman.

I needed to exercise my body to awaken my muscles, which were coming back to life. I wanted to look as different as I felt. I bought new glasses to show my eyes more and wore less make-up. I didn't want to hide my face. I wanted to maintain the honesty I had found in my "peach fuzz" days.

I also had to readjust to the outside world; in other words, I had to socialize. Lydia threw a "silly hat" party at which I had to fight the urge to jump on a chair and say, "Hey, I just recovered from cancer!" But with the help of my family and friends I could finally have a conversation and not mention the lymphoma. I told Fran this on one of our many "art nights" out, and she responded, "It must be hard not to mention it, though." It helped to be in public with someone who had shared my experience, and to have company in my silences.

I realized the lymphoma would always be with me. I had fought death and could not pretend nothing had happened; I just needed to incorporate the experience into my life.

I decided to pay a social visit to Dr. Douglas. After we conversed awhile in his office and I showed photos of my latest work, we hugged goodbye as usual. Just before I left, I turned and asked if I could visit again.

"Sure, anytime. I'm always here," he replied.

Suddenly I felt happy. Losing his friendship would have upset me greatly. But I did not and our friendship grew.

The two months between my first and second periods were absolute hell. It was the longest PMS I ever had. Unfortunately my mother and Julia bore the brunt of it. My mother got Darcy-the-grouch every morning. She swears she doesn't remember my two-month morning crab face, but that's just her being charitable. Julia got the woe-is-me Darcy. We met for lunch often; I would sit and moan about not getting into a gallery, trouble with my period, and not meeting a guy. I felt like I had "damaged goods" written across my chest. Julia brushed these comments aside and encouraged me not to give up.

S*pring: Ascent to My New Life* ⮁ Spring came with another period. I began to climb out of my depression. I reflected deeply on my brush with death and my rebirth, and now felt blessed by this experience. I discovered what a gift it is to be alive. I also realized that a lot of my depression was due to those damned hormones. The trauma from the tumor, nearly dying, and treatment had been enormous. I had to respect that and ride with it.

I completed a triptych for my recovery: *Return of Myself Anew* **[PLATE 18]**. It was done over the three months of depression, and each panel shows a different stage of recovery. **PLATE A** is me returning to the well world. **PLATE B** is me in the midst of my depression. PLATE C is my new-found self and knowledge. I painted the seals translucent, for they are preparing to leave me because I no longer need them.

In April I paid a social visit to Dr. Leonard.

"Wow, your hair is really growing!" he exclaimed.

"Yes, I'm waiting for it to obey the laws of gravity." It had grown slightly darker and was curly.

"May I?" he gestured with one hand over my head.

"Sure, I do it all the time!"

"Pretty thick, huh?" He ruffled it. "But I liked the punk look too" (meaning my peach fuzz).

I showed Dr. Leonard photos of my latest work and we chatted. From there I went to see Dr. Barnes; I had an appointment for a checkup.

"You are sans Hickman now," Dr. Barnes said, grinning over his desk.

"I knew I forgot something!" I said, looking under my sweater.

"That reminds me of a Hickman joke." He proceeded to tell me a long-winded joke that I thought was just dreadful.

Return of Myself Anew
[Plate 18, page 110]
Oil on canvas. January-March 1992. Each panel 16" x 24"

"'Beam me up' is better." I grimaced. "But it never worked, so I returned it to Dr. Leonard."

"Yeah, that's a good one. Any luck with the paintings?"

"No, nobody has the guts to show them. But I won't give up."

"That's good. How are you feeling?"

"OK . . . but I'm still tired all the time."

"It takes a long time to recover. Let me examine you." After finishing he said, "You are fine. See me in three months."

"Three months? Won't you miss me?"

"Yeah." We hugged and I went home.

Spring was a glorious explosion of color. Colors and scents were totally fresh and new; I painted many landscapes. I continued to search for ways to get my lymphoma work shown. At one of our lunches together, Lydia said, "Why don't you turn it into a book? It would be much more accessible and personal then."

"Nah, I can't write."

Epilogue

Needless to say, I followed Lydia's advice and this is the result. It was quite an awakening. I now have a new view on life, and focus on what I believe to be most important: love, creativity, and survival.

My relationships with family and friends reached a higher level of honesty, and many of the bonds strengthened. I acquired new friends: Dr. Barnes, Dr. Leonard, Dr. Blake, Nurse Helen, Nurse Kate, and of course, Dr. Douglas.

I learned much about myself that helped me move forward in life. I found a sense of self-worth and an appreciation of my body. I will never disregard it again.

I found a powerful connection to my grandfather, Burt Johnson, a sculptor who died of a heart attack at the age of 37. I saw much of his work in California, just before my return to New York, and discovered the roots of my creativity. While in the hospital I thought of him often and felt he was "up there" looking out for me, making sure I would survive because he did not. I never had any intention of dying, but now it was time to start living.

I have grown self-absorbed and self-referential, and am always searching for higher forms of art that express the intensity of life. My own art has benefited from my having had cancer, and I try to put as much honesty and depth into it as possible.

I am often reminded of the words from a John Lennon song: "Life is what happens to you while you are busy making other plans." Life has become exciting and enjoyable, and my art goes on.

The Lymphoma Series

The following paintings are what I call *The Lymphoma Series*, which I painted during my illness, treatment, and recovery from the cancer, lymphoma. There are four categories:

Images From the Hospital
My Body During Treatment
Portraits
Recovery

Under each painting is a brief caption to explain how the painting fits into my experience.

PLATE 1
Pieta/Start of the Climb

After surgery and diagnosis, this is the image I saw
of my doctors rescuing me from a sewer of lymphoma.

Oil on canvas. June 1991. 24" x 18"

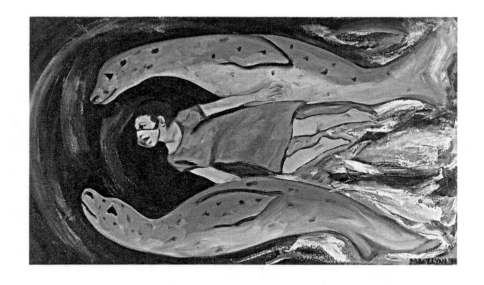

PLATE 2
Seals I

This is the image I had while in intensive care on oxygen. The chest tube in me added to the effect, as it made bubbling sounds like those heard underwater.

Oil on canvas. June 1991. 28" x 16"

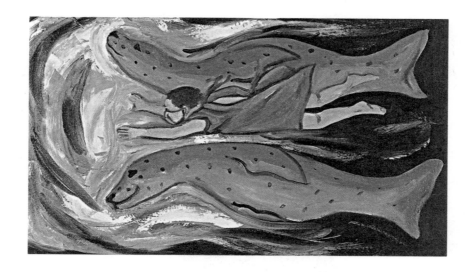

PLATE 3
Seals II

I painted this image twice, as it was such a positive and uplifting one.

A reminder that life is a gift.

Oil on canvas. July 1991. 28" x 16"

PLATE 4
The Illusion in the X-Ray Room

I was in my wheelchair waiting to return to my room
when I thought I saw death pass me, but it was
only the resident rabbi walking by.

Oil on canvas. September 1991. 16" x 22"

PLATE 5

The Hospital Nightmare

Everyone has one. This was Dr. Loblolly chasing me down a
dark hallway on a wooden platform, his long arms frozen at his
sides and a manic grin on his face.

Oil on canvas. July 1991. 16" x 24"

PLATE 6
In the Garden

Late one night in the hospital I saw myself in a gray and misty garden,
alone among the statues, feeling emptiness and solitude.

Oil on canvas. June 1991. 24" x 18"

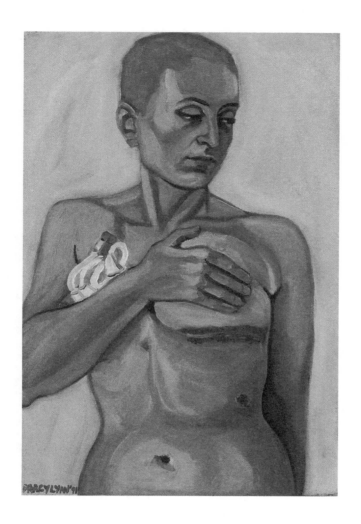

Self-Portrait With Hickman and Scar

My dear friend Julia said, "Paint everything."
Part of that was to face my scars and know that I am alive.

Oil on canvas. July 1991. 16" x 24"

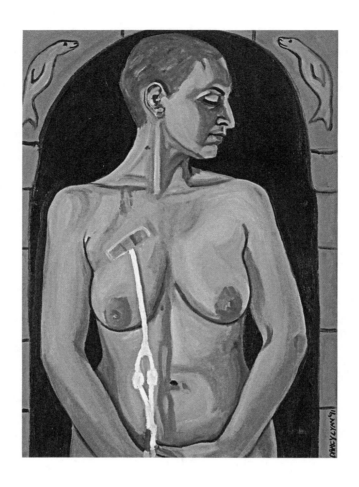

PLATE 8
Self-Portrait/Reflection

After my Hickman catheter was put in place
I saw my reflection in the lights above. I looked very vulnerable.
How to maintain one's dignity through it all.

Oil on canvas. August 1991. 20" x 28"

PLATE 9
My Dramatic Body

Throughout treatment my body reacted in extremes.
Dr. Douglas said I had a dramatic body. Also, the effects of
chemotherapy put my body in a state of turmoil.

Oil on canvas. August 1991. 18" x 28"

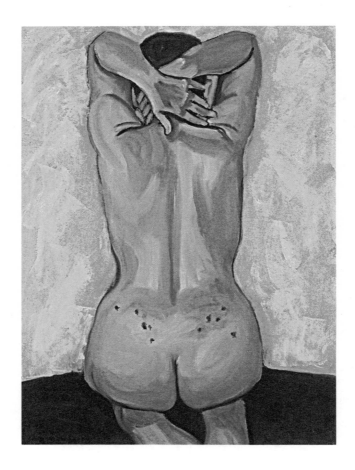

PLATE 10
After the Harvest

Before radiation could start I had a bone marrow harvest,
a procedure of removing white blood cells from the hip bone to store
in case the lymphoma returns and a transplant is needed.

Oil on canvas. November 1991. 16" x 22"

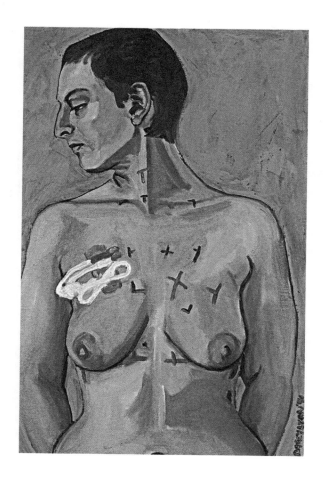

PLATE 11
Self-Portrait With Radiation Tattoos

My radiation treatment lasted six weeks;
the tattoos indicate where I got "zapped."
Fuchsia was for the first 8 zaps; blue for the final 16 zaps.

Oil on canvas. November 1991. 14" x 22"

PLATE 12

Rebirth

Self-explanatory.

Oil on canvas. August 1991. 18" x 24"

PLATE 13
Friends Triptych (Fran, Darcy, Julia)

*This very intense group portrait of myself and my friends symbolizes
the support they gave me during my illness. I also wanted to
capture the look in their eyes as they saw me in the hospital.*

Oil on canvas. August 1991. Each panel: 14" x 20"

PLATE 14

Nurse Helen

I was in the hospital clinic for three weeks
with an unidentified infection, kept on intravenous antibiotics.
Nurse Helen kept me sane and smiling.
A very special lady and a wonderful nurse.

Oil on canvas. August 1991. 16" x 20"

PLATE 15
Doctor Triptych
(Dr. Barnes, Dr. Douglas, Dr. Leonard)

*Here I tried to convey the fear of the unknown by the dark background
with the very real presence of my doctors. In the pillars are symbols
of each one from my sketches in the hospital and a seal for hope.
I was fortunate to have such intelligent, caring, and modest doctors
to help me fight lymphoma emotionally as well as physically.*

Oil on canvas. July 1991. Each panel 20" x 28"

PLATE 16
Doctor Blake

My last doctor, my radiologist. An energetic, cautious, caring doctor.
*She is in a similar setting to that in **Doctor Triptych***
except that she has her own niche.

Oil on canvas. December 1991. 20" x 28"

PLATE 17
The Three Musketeers

I got this idea in the hospital when I told Dr. Leonard I was going to
paint all three of them. He said they were the three musketeers.
Also, laughter is the best medicine.

Oil on canvas. September 1991. 24" x 18"

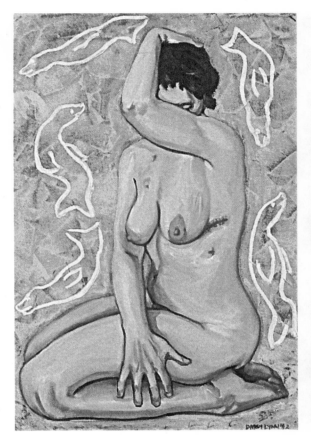

PLATE 18
Return of Myself Anew

*After my recovery my Hickman catheter was removed in January 1992,
and of course my hair was growing back. Emotionally, I was still recovering
from the impact and ordeal. This triptych shows my slow return of body and
soul, but with a discovery of the joy of life.*

Oil on canvas. January–March 1992. Each panel 16" x 24"

PLATE **19**

Brooklyn Botanical Gardens

Nature became a great source of comfort and reassurance

of life to me during my illness. It still is.

Oil on canvas. September 1991. 30" x 20"